Bonsai

The Complete Step-by-Step Guide for Beginners

HIKARU YAMASAKI

BONSAI

© Copyright 2019 - All rights reserved.

The content contained within this book may not be reproduced, duplicated or transmitted without direct written permission from the author or the publisher.

Under no circumstances will any blame or legal responsibility be held against the publisher, or author, for any damages, reparation, or monetary loss due to the information contained within this book. Either directly or indirectly.

Legal Notice:

This book is copyright protected. This book is only for personal use. You cannot amend, distribute, sell, use, quote or paraphrase any part, or the content within this book, without the consent of the author or publisher.

Disclaimer Notice:

Please note the information contained within this document is for educational and entertainment purposes only. All effort has been executed to present accurate, up to date, and reliable, complete information. No warranties of any kind are declared or implied. Readers acknowledge that the author is not engaging in the rendering of legal, financial, medical or professional advice. The content within this book has been derived from various sources. Please consult a licensed professional before attempting any techniques outlined in this book.

By reading this document, the reader agrees that under no circumstances is the author responsible for any losses, direct or indirect, which are incurred as a result of the use of information contained within this document, including, but not limited to, — errors, omissions, or inaccuracies.

Table of Contents

INTRODUCTION VIII
CHAPTER 1 THE ORIGIN AND HISTORY OF BONSAI 1
- History of Bonsai in China 2
- History of Bonsai in Japan 3
- History of Bonsai in the Western World 6

CHAPTER 2 BASIC BONSAI STYLES 9
- How Bonsai Styles Determines the Selection of Your Container 10
  - *Bonsai Style 1: The "Chokkan" or the Formal Upstanding* 10
  - *Bonsai Style 2: Informal Upright or "Moyogi"* 12
  - *Bonsai Style 3: Slanting or "Shakan"* 14
  - *Bonsai Style 4: Cascade or "Kengai"* 15
  - *Bonsai Style 5: Semi-Cascade or "Han-Kengai"* 16
- More Bonsai Styles 17
  - *Windswept or "Fukinagashi"* 18
  - *Literati Style or "Bunjingi"* 18
- Other Styles of Bonsai That Spring from the Five Basic Styles 19
  - *Broom Style or "Hokidachi"* 20
  - *Exposed-Root Style* 20
  - *Root-over-Rock Style or "Seki-joju"* 21
  - *Growing-on-a-Rock Style or "Seki-joju"* 23
  - *Double-Trunk Style or "Sokan"* 24
  - *Clump Style* 25
  - *Raft Style or "Ikadabuki"* 26
  - *Forest Style or "Yose-ue"* 26
  - *Weeping Style* 27
  - *Shari Bonsai Style ("Sharimiki")* 28

CHAPTER 3 TYPES OF BONSAI 29

CHAPTER 4 SELECTING A BONSAI TREE 34
- Size 34
- The Surroundings Where It Will be Placed 35
- Grower's Experience 35
- Buying a Healthy Tree 36
- Structural Features 36

Bonsai Material 38
　　Outdoor or Indoor Bonsai Tree? 38

CHAPTER 5 THE VITAL TOOLS 40

　　Shears and Pliers 41
　　Knives and Saws 42
　　Tools for Roots and Repotting 42
　　Tools for Wiring 43
　　Tools for Bending (and Protective Materials) 44
　　Tools and Carving Knives for Deadwood 45
　　Other Bonsai Tools 45
　　Electronic Bonsai Tools 46
　　Materials and Tools for Maintenance 48
　　Watering Tools and Systems 48
　　Turntables 49
　　Tool Maintenance 50
　　What to Buy 50

CHAPTER 6 CULTIVATION 52

　　Bonsai Soil 53
　　　　Soil pH 53
　　　　Soil Size 54
　　　　Making Soil 55
　　　　Putting Soil in the Pot 55
　　　　Muck 56
　　Bonsai Cultivation Techniques 57
　　　　Growing Bonsai from Seed 57
　　　　Growing Bonsai from Cuttings 62
　　　　Growing Bonsai from Nursery Stock / Pre-Bonsai 63
　　　　Growing Bonsai from Collecting Trees (Yamadori) 64
　　　　Buying Bonsai Trees 66
　　Choosing Your Tree 66
　　The Cheapest and Nicest Ways 67

CHAPTER 7 PRUNING AND TRIMMING 69

　　Pruning Bonsai 69
　　　　Bonsai Maintenance Pruning 70
　　　　Structural Bonsai Pruning 71
　　Growth Principles 73

CHAPTER 8 WIRING 78

ATTITUDE 78
WHY SPIRAL WIRE? 78
THINKING AHEAD 80
TIMING 81
ALUMINUM VERSUS COPPER WIRE 82
WIRE THICKNESS 82
WIRING SEQUENCE 83
HOW LONG DO YOU CUT THE WIRE? 83
ADEQUATE ANCHORING 83
THE SPIRALING PROCESS 84
CARE AFTER WIRING 85
WHEN DO YOU TAKE THE WIRE OFF? 86
FINALLY 86

CHAPTER 9 WATERING AND FERTILIZING 87

WATERING 87
FERTILIZER 89
   NPK *89*
   A Balanced Fertilizer *90*
   Macronutrients and Micronutrient *90*
   When Should You Fertilize? *91*
   What Kind Fertilizer Should You Use? *91*
   How Much Fertilizer to Use *93*
   When to Change the Fertilizer? *93*
   Chlorosis: Yellowing of Leaves *94*
   Too Much Fertilizer *94*

CHAPTER 10 SEASONAL CARE 96

WHAT MAKES A GOOD BONSAI 96
BEFORE BONSAI TRAINING 97
AFTER DRASTIC PRUNING AND POTTING 98
WINTER-TIME CARE FOR BONSAI TREES 99
   Normal Wintering *100*
   Below Fifteen Degrees *100*
   Watering and Fertilizer *101*
   Tropical and Subtropical Bonsai *101*
SUMMER BONSAI TREE CARE 102
   Temperature *102*
   Humidity *102*
   Growth *103*

CARING FOR AN EVERGREEN BONSAI TREE	103
Watering	*103*
Fertilizing	*104*
Pruning	*104*
Sunlight	*104*
RULES OF BONSAI	105
Trunk and Nebari Rules	*105*
Branches	*106*
Pots	*108*
Culture	*109*

CHAPTER 11 REPOTTING 110

WHY REPOT YOUR BONSAI?	110
ROOT BOUND	111
WHAT ARE THE SIGNS THAT A BONSAI NEEDS REPOTTING?	112
WHICH PERIOD OF THE YEAR IS PERFECT FOR REPOTTING?	113
WHAT'S THE DEAL WITH WAITING?	113
THE BEST TIME IS NOW!	114
SUMMER AND FALL REPOTTING	114
PROCEDURE FOR REPOTTING A BONSAI TREE	115
Highlights of Female versus Male Highlights of a Bonsai Tree	*115*
Step 1. Choosing a Pot	*116*
Step 2: Preparing the New Pot	*117*
Step 3: Relocating the Tree to the New Pot	*118*
Step 4: Check the Angle and Find the Front	*118*
Step 5: Fastening and Introducing Fresh Soil	*119*
Step 6: Finishing	*119*
Step 7: Watering the Tree	*119*

CHAPTER 12 PRESENTING YOUR BONSAI 121

MONO NO AWARE	122
WABI-SABI	122
Miniaturization	*123*
Proportions among the Various Elements	*124*
Symmetry versus Asymmetry	*124*
Absence of Traces	*125*
Poignancy	*125*
THE IMPORTANCE OF THE PRESENTATION OF BONSAI	126
The Front Side of a Bonsai Tree	*127*
The Appropriate Height of Showcasing a Bonsai Tree	*127*

Emphasizing the Beauty of Bonsai by Removing All Clutter.................................*128*
INCREASING THE AESTHETIC APPEAL OF AN EVERGREEN BONSAI.............129

CONCLUSION START GROWING A BONSAI NOW....................... 132

INTRODUCTION

Bonsai is an ancient art of planting that originated from the Eastern World but is well adopted in the West. It's quite puzzling and raises suspicion at first sight. At times it could be a passing interest that eventually fades with time, but in some instances, some individuals take their time to make more research about this beautiful piece of mini-gardening method.

They are different from short trees and other plants that are grown in containers. They are full-sized trees and are planted using basic bonsai methods, such as potting, pruning, wiring, root reduction, defoliation, etc. Generally speaking, bonsai are planted and left to grow in containers, pots, and trays.

Bonsai is more than just planting. It is a form of therapy and enhances fine qualities, such as patience and mental strength, and it also helps in relaxing the mind. For the early Chinese, a tree could be the connection between heaven and earth, and between the holy and the human. Thus, they had a popular belief that those who nurtured a miniature tree for long will be granted eternal life. To them, the trees are not nurtured for the production of medicine and food but mainly for landscaping and aesthetics.

The trees could be of different shapes and styles, either formal or informal, for example, cascade, slant, windswept, etc. The planting pots could be simple or unusually shaped trays made of wood, stone, plastic, or ceramic. There are special pots that are used for planting bonsai. These pots have small drainage holes in their base to allow excess water to drain out of the pot. Also, these holes have meshes to support the roots till the tree is matured enough and can carry its own weight, and to prevent soil from falling out.

BONSAI

According to ancient records, the Chinese were the first set of people to grow bonsai. But, the Japanese made significant efforts by developing and improving it, giving the art the modern touch we all see today. Bonsai are not genetically dwarfed plants as most people assume it to be, rather, their growth is inhibited by a number of methods and stages that, if done properly, would enable the tree to live as long as other wild trees of the same species. One interesting thing is that a vast variety of trees can be grown as bonsai.

This book contains all you need to know about bonsai and the techniques to enable them to grow.

Chapter 1

The Origin and History of Bonsai

The art of bonsai originated in the Chinese empire. However, the word "bon-sai" is coined from the Japanese language. As far back as AD 700, the Chinese had commenced the art of *pun-tsai*, as it was called, using special methods to grow trees in containers. Back then, only the rich and influential of the society could afford to practice the art of pun-tsai, using locally-collected materials. The trees were so valuable that they could be given as valuable gifts in China.

The period known as the Kamakura period was the period in which Japan adopted most of China's customs. The art of growing trees in containers was adopted as well by the Japanese. The Japanese did not just adopt the art but also developed bonsai due to two main reasons which were the influence of Zen Buddhism and the small size of Japan, which is about 4 percent the size of China's mainland. Thus, the landscape was quite small and very limited. A number of popular styles, methods, and tools were invented in Japan from Chinese originals. For about three centuries, the art was known to be limited to the provinces of Asia. Only recently has bonsai truly been spread to other continents.

History of Bonsai in China

Various shallow basins or flattened bowls made out of earthenware, such as "pen" or "pan" or "pun," had been made in what we now know as China since about five thousand years ago. A millennium later, during the Chinese bronze age, these shapes were selected among the shapes to be recreated in bronze for political and religious ceremonial purposes. There is a theory that was widely believed by the Chinese—the five elements theory: *fire, soil, water, wood, earth, and metal.* This theory, which was popular about 2,300 years ago, spread the idea about the potency of replicas in miniature. For example, by recreating a mountain, on a smaller scale, a student could focus on its magical potential and have access to them. The more the replica was in size from the original, the more its magical potent was likely to be.

About two hundred years later, under the Han emperor, importations of new aromatics and incenses were allowed due to newly opened trading with nearby nations. There was a new type of vessel made. The vessel took the form of two mountain peaks. These peaks were made above the waves and represent the dwelling of the immortals, the mythic islands of the blessed. The vessel was used for burning sweet-smelling fragrance (incense). Initially crafted out of ceramic, bronze, or overlaid with bronze, some of these burners were braced on small pen dishes to either hold a miniature symbolic ocean or to collect hot embers. The detachable cover or lids to these burners were designed in style to represent some legendary figures climbing the sides of a forested mountain. Through the holes in the lids, the incense smoke arose out of the cave openings having the appearance of the mystic vapors in the original-sized mountains. Some removable covers made out of stone may have been found with lichens around it. These covers depict small-scale natural landscapes.

Sometime in AD 706 came the tomb paintings for Crowned Prince Zhang Huai, which portrayed artistic rendition of two ladies-in-waiting, offering small-sized stony scenes with little plants in shallow trays. At that time, more advancement was made in the invention and care of bonsai tree while the development of the art was also taking place. By this time, there were already early written depictions of these pun-wan (tray playthings).

The earliest discovered and then containerized trees were assumed to have been specially-shaped and twisted trees from the wild. These were "holy" instead of "profane" because the trees could not be used for any food, medicine, or ordinary purposes, such as lumber. Their unusual forms were similar to yoga-type body position which twisted back on itself in a repeated manner so that vital fluids can keep flowing. This was believed to be responsible for long life.

For centuries, various regional styles would be developed all over the great country, China, with its many landscapes. Porcelain displayed on wooden stands would be replaced with earthenware and ceramic containers, and attempts would be made to reshape the trees using bamboo frameworks, brass wire, or lead strips. Many writers and poets each described at least one tree and/or mountainous miniature landscapes, and many artists included a dwarfed potted tree as a sign of a cultivated man's lifestyle. At the end of the sixteenth century, these were called *pun-tsai* or "tray planting." Not until the seventeenth century did the word *pun ching* ("tray landscape," now called *penjing*) actually come into usage.

History of Bonsai in Japan

BONSAI

It is widely accepted that the first tray landscapes were transported from China to Japan, at least 1,200 of them (as religious items). A millennium ago, the first extensive work of fiction in Japanese included this line, "A [big-sized] tree that is allowed to grow under its natural condition is a crude thing. It is only when it is grown close to human beings who nurture it with loving care that its style and shape acquire the capacity to move one."

The first graphical depictions of these in Japan were not made until about eight hundred years ago. All the things made by the Chinese amazed the Japanese, and it was only a matter of time before the Chinese Chan Buddhism (native Chinese Daoism combined with Indian meditative Dhyana Buddhism) was also imported, and it became known as Zen Buddhism in Japan. With limited landforms as a model, Zen monks were able to design their plate along specific lines, such that just one potted tree could portray our universe, and one could find beauty in something as small as a bonsai.

The Japanese pots were made a bit deeper than those from China, and the resulting gardening style was named *hachi-no-ki,* which literally meant "the bowl's tree." A story from the late 1300s, about a poor samurai who had to burn the last three surviving bonsai trees to provide warmth to a monk on voyage because it was winter and the night was so cold, was later adopted as a popular noh theatre play. Images from the story were later portrayed in a number of forms, including woodblock prints through the years.

Everybody, from the military leader to common artisans, grew different forms of the tree in a pot, tray, or abalone shell. By the late eighteenth century, an event to showcase traditional pine-dwarf potted trees commenced and were to be held annually in the capital city of Kyoto. Specialists from the neighboring areas and five provinces would bring one or two plants each for display in order to showcase them to the visitors for scoring or judging. As a major source of income, Takamatsu province (where Kinashi Bonsai

Village could be found) was already into the business of making potted pines.

By 1800, a group of learned Chinese gathered around near the city of Osaka to discuss recent methods of growing dwarf trees. Their miniature trees were renamed as *"bonsai"* (which is a Japanese term that replaced the Chinese pronunciation, *pun-tsai)* as a way of separating them from the common *hachi-no-ki,* which most people nurtured. The pen or bon is not as deep as the *hachi* bowl. This proves one point—that some cultivators were more successful with the horticultural needs of miniature trees in small-sized pots. By then, bonsai was viewed as a form of art. The craft's technique was replacing the mythical and religious approach to customs.

A variety of styles and sizes were invented over a hundred years. Books and journals that gave details on the tools, pots, and the tree itself were printed. Various events were held as well. Hemp fibers were replaced with iron and copper wire for shaping the trees. Flower containers mass-produced in China and to be transported to Japan were made with strict specifications, and a number of people grew them as a form of hobby.

In 1923, a great earthquake, known as Kanto, affected a large part of Tokyo. After the earthquake, about thirty families who were skilled bonsai enthusiasts relocated to Omiya, which was about twenty miles away from Tokyo, and there, with time, Omiya village became the heart of Japanese bonsai traditions. Around the 1930s, official annual events were held at Tokyo's Metropolitan Museum of Art. At that time, the Omiya bonsai art has gained much popularity.

The long recovery from the Pacific War made bonsai become developed and cultivated as an important native art. Training, more events for the display of potted trees, journals and articles, and classes for foreigners further popularized the art of bonsai. The use of traditional power tools, along with a deep knowledge of plant physiology, enabled a few skilled trainers to move from the traditional method to a more artistic-designing phase of the art.

In recent times, bonsai is perceived more often as just a way of keeping the elderly busy. However, the art is gaining more popularity among the youth, with the availability of native, easy-to-care-for dwarf trees, which have beautiful scenes, without meshes, and look wild.

History of Bonsai in the Western World

In 1604, there was a depiction in Spanish of how Chinese settlers in the tropical islands of the Philippines were culturing small ficus trees onto hand-sized bits of coral. The first record of English observation of short trees planted in pots (a root surrounded by rocks in a pot) in Macau/China was in 1637. Thereafter, reports following the next century, likewise from Japan, were root-in-rock samples. Dozens of voyagers mentioned some of the potted trees in their reports from China or Japan. A considerable number of these were restated in literature reviews and excerpts from articles that had worldwide distribution. In 1893, the Japanese potted trees were in the Philadelphia exhibition, also in Paris exhibition in 1878 and 1889 respectively. It was also on display during the Chicago Exposition of 1893, St. Louis World's Fair of 1904, 1910 Britain-Japan Exhibition, and also at the 1915 San Francisco Expo.

The first-known European dialect book (French) that focused completely on Japanese potted trees was printed in 1902, but the English version was not published until 1940. In 1957, Yoshimura and Halford's *Miniature Trees and Landscapes* were published. It was later known as the "Bible of Bonsai in the West," with Yuji Yoshimura being the link between Japanese traditional bonsai art and the developing Western approach, which resulted in a refined adoption for the present world. Also, the efforts of John Naka, who was from California, further popularized the art by teaching it in print and in person, first in America and then in other parts of the world, further emphasizing the use of traditional material.

It was during this period that the Western world became acquainted with the beautiful arts (landscape) from China called *penjing,* while resurgence and *saikei* were from Japan. A combination of more than two or more types of trees became popular and accepted as a legit invention.

Over the years, little improvements and modifications have been made, mainly in the ancient bonsai nurseries in Japan, and these updates have been extended to our countries by returning travel enthusiasts or visiting teachers. Upon arriving in Japan, at various workshops right in the presence of students, instructors would promptly try out one or two new techniques. These new techniques from Japan can be passed to others thereafter, and thus, this living art form continued to be developed.

A lot of the books written in the English language focused more on fundamental horticultural methods and techniques for keeping the trees alive. Western education has helped in broadening our knowledge on the requirements and stages involved in the growth and survival of trees and other plants in our compositions. In addition, published journals have moved their focus to explain the processes involved in shaping and styling. Many collections of miniature trees began to be collected and stored in different countries around the world, such as Hungary, Australia, Scotland, and Korea, and a number of events, exhibitions, and conventions are held annually for tree-lovers and other interested members of the public.

It was around this time that "mica pots" originated in Korea, and independent potters experimented with various ceramic pots,

BONSAI

including substandard designs. The first bonsai website was launched in 1992. It began with the *alt.bonsai* newsgroup, then the following year, the first online bonsai club was launched, *rec.arts.bonsai*. And in less than three years, the first official bonsai club website was set up.

One movie that inspired many young ones to investigate the art was *The Karate Kid*.

At present, we have over 1,200 books written in about twenty-six dialects that focus on bonsai and closely related arts. Also, there are over fifty yearly print journals in various languages and five online articles simply in English. Dozens of websites, club newsletters, over a hundred discussion forums online and in blogs can be studied. With continuous references on TV, in movies and adverts, and in science fiction and non-fiction works, indeed, the interest is rising globally. There are also an estimated one thousand clubs meeting in various countries two-three times a month, all with their own style of politics, personalities, and passions. Membership might have risen close to a hundred thousand in over a hundred countries and territories, with non-associated bonsai lovers totaling perhaps ten million more.

So the next time you prune a branch, wire it, or repot your tree, think deeply about what you are doing. You are prolonging over a thousand-year legacy. Personally, you are creating a small version of your

Chapter 2

Basic Bonsai Styles

When molding a bonsai tree, the initial step is to choose which style is most appropriate to the tree's natural structure. While there are intricate varieties of shapes and styles from which to pick, bonsai is normally grouped into five essential styles:

- formal upright
- informal upright
- slanting
- cascade
- semi-cascade

These groupings depend on the general state of the tree and how much the storage compartment or trunk slants away from an imaginary vertical line. There are two extra styles (literati and windswept) that are usually considered as basic styles.

How Bonsai Styles Determines the Selection of Your Container

Just before you plant that tree in the pot, pause for a moment and think about how it will grow in the pot. Take a while to imagine placement before making a move. This helps prevent the common mistake that usually leads to a tree planted one way and then removed to make an adjustment.

Remember your general goal when planting bonsai. Upright trees ought to have a balanced look in the pot. Slanted and cascaded styles frequently have their upper root surfaces exposed to mimic the way plants grow naturally.

Regardless of what style you pick, whether a single-trunk tree or groups of trees from single roots, everything relies on your choice of plant material and your capacity to imagine the bonsai's final shape.

Bonsai Style 1: The "Chokkan" or the Formal Upstanding

The formal upstanding style is the easiest for a beginner to develop because it has classic proportions and is the basis of all bonsai. This is because of the following reasons:

- It requires minimal experimentation.
- It prevents the challenge of selective pruning.
- It should almost immediately become a presentable bonsai.

In this method, the shape is in the form of a cone or circle while the tree is upright, and the branches are leveled. Basically, one of the branches is lower and broadens a little away from the trunk when compared to the others. In addition, the last two branches are primed to grow forward on the front side of the tree, one a bit higher than the other. The third branch of this extends to the rear of the other tree at a point just between the two side branches in a way that gives the plant depth.

When choosing a nursery plant for this style, search for a tree with a trunk that ascends from the root in a relatively straight line. Also, the trunk ought to be single, without forks. An even distribution of branches is also imperative. The first branch ought to be the most developed and positioned, at roughly one-third of the way up the tree's trunk.

At first, shape by cutting off the little twigs or branches that are very close to the ground and near the major stem. These branches deviate from the general arrangement. The objective is to build up a feeling of balance, however, not strict symmetry.

This method is most appropriate to conifers. Fruiting informal trees are not fit for formal upright.

Appropriate Containers: Trees in the formal upstanding style look best in oval or rectangular holders. For satisfying proportions, abstain from centering the tree in the pot. Rather, place it about one-third of the distance from one end.

Recommended Species: Junipers, pines, larches, and spruces are all good species for formal upright bonsai. Maples may likewise be used. However, they are not as easy to prime and shape.

Bonsai Style 2: Informal Upright or "Moyogi"

The informal upright style is a very common style, a fundamental design that follows the natural form of the tree's trunk. The aim is to have a single line of the trunk, rising from the roots to the top while growing a good foliage structure and natural branch.

The trunk in this second style curves slightly to the front. A number of nursery trees are slanted by nature, making them appropriate for the informal upright style. Examine the tree's slant by taking a downward look at the trunk from above. From this vantage point, the top is expected to slant forward.

BONSAI

Assuming the view from above is not alluring, you may move the root-ball to incline the tree on another path. Just repot the tree, slanting the plant in its new pot. When this is done, take a minute to examine the tree. Take into consideration if the branches and leaves need to be trimmed to make them proportionate to the size of the tree.

As with the formal upright method, the branching begins at about one-third of the way up. Search for a tree with few spaces or, if any, empty spaces.

In the informal upright style, rather than being erect as in the formal upright style, the apex bends slightly to the front. This bend further gives the style a feeling of informality and makes the branches appears as if they were in motion.

Appropriate Containers: This informal method is more adorable in an oval or rectangular container. Place a one-third of the distance from one end of the container and not in the middle.

BONSAI

Recommended Species: A lot of species of plants are fit for this style, primarily trident maple (*Acer buergerianum*), the Japanese maple (*Acer palmatum*), beech, practically all conifers, and other adorable trees, such as the cotoneaster, crab apple, and pomegranate.

Bonsai Style 3: Slanting or "Shakan"

In nature, slanting trees are called "leaners," trees that have been constrained by gravity and the wind into nonvertical development. Inclined- or slanted-style trees often give an incredible impression of age and strength.

In the slanting bonsai style, the trunk is more angular than in the other methods. The apex of the tree slants forward slightly.

The least branch should extend to the opposite direction in which the tree slants. The branches closer to the base are arranged in groups of three, starting about one-third of the way up the trunk.

The manner the slanting style takes fall between the upright and cascade styles. The goal of the slanting style or "shakan" is to find a middle ground between the movement of the trunk and the placement of the branches, so the tree would not appear unbalanced.

Appropriate Containers: This method will appear more beautiful if it is planted in the center of a square or circular pot.

Recommended Species: A lot of species are fit for this style because the style is quite similar to the informal upright. Conifers are also a good choice as well.

Bonsai Style 4: Cascade or "Kengai"

The cascade pattern of bonsai depicts a natural tree growing down the surface of an embankment.

In this bonsai style, the trunk begins to grow upward from the soil, then turns downward suddenly, and gets to a point below the base at the edge of the container. For that, the container should be kept close to the tip of a small table or flat stand.

The cascade method has most of its leaves below the soil surface.

Nurturing a tree using the cascade style takes a longer time than the slanting style. To obtain a better result, choose a low-growing species rather than forcing a tree that naturally grows upright into an unnatural shape. Curve the entire tree forward such that the side branches fall naturally and one branch turns back vertically, in a cascading manner.

Appropriate Containers: A tree planted with this style is more attractive in a round or hexagonal container that is high but not so wide.

Recommended Species: All the species that can be used for bonsai are suitable for cascade styles. Most wide leaves, such as the ficus and virtually all deciduous species, will make a beautiful cascade style. Conifers are also often styled as cascades.

Bonsai Style 5: Semi-Cascade or "Han-Kengai"

The semi-cascade method portrays a tree trunk that is made to grow upward for a specific distance and then is cascaded in a downward manner at a less angular point, less than in the cascade style. The semi-cascade method has a curving bark that does not get to the base of the container, unlike that of the cascade style.

The cascading branches are assumed to be the front of the tree, and the back branches are primed closer to the trunk than others.

Branches, as well as leaves, in the semi-cascade ought not to extend beneath the base of the pot but are beneath the surface of the soil.

Appropriate Containers: A large proportion of semi-cascade pots are a bit deeper than their length and width. The most preferred shapes are square, round, and hexagonal.

Recommended Species: Plants that are well suited to the cascade and semi-cascade styles include the ornamental plants, such as chrysanthemums, wisteria, willows, star, and jasmine prostrate junipers.

More Bonsai Styles

Windswept or "Fukinagashi"

This style enhances the effect of continuous exposure to strong winds. In this style, each of the branches seems to be "swept" to one side, in such a way that it appears to be being blown by a strong breeze or having large parts of the branches and leaves become affected by exposure to harsh environmental conditions.

These trees are primed after trees that grow in coastal and mountainous regions, where strong natural forces have molded and formed them naturally for years.

Literati Style or "Bunjingi"

The literati style of bonsai was initially designed to portray the importance of a tree. A literati has an adorable, sleek, and specialized trunk line. Only a limited number of branches are allowed. This style is often believed to be the most challenging to achieve. It is only bonsai enthusiasts that have mastered all the principles and created spectacular designs in the past that can successfully break the classic rules and create beautiful literati.

Other Styles of Bonsai That Spring from the Five Basic Styles

Broom Style or "Hokidachi"

The broom-style bonsai is similar to the old trees that grow along city streets or in plantations. A deciduous plant species is primed to form radial branches or a crown that show a lot of ramification (branching twigs), thereby forming a beautiful appearance of an old tree. Some broom styles have branches radiating from one central point while others have a major trunk axis that rises from the base of the trunk to the apex.

Exposed-Root Style

BONSAI

Naturally, weather and rain can wash away the soil from the root of a tree, gradually exposing its roots after some years. Bonsai enthusiasts are fond of exaggerating this effect and portray a large portion of root structure. This effect can be achieved after a long time by exposing only a bit of the root yearly and letting the exposed portion harden off.

Root-over-Rock Style or "Seki-joju"

BONSAI

When a seed falls in an opening on a rock and gains access to sufficient soil to survive, the plant's roots may extend further and spread across the thin layers of moss and soil across the rock. In another instance, the roots could gradually grow over the surface of the rock and extend till it reaches soil below, in a way that it eventually encases the rock. This effect in bonsai can be created by spreading roots over a rock and waiting till the roots develop. To achieve this, bury the rock among the roots during the process of planting the plant in the pot, and allow it to grow for some years before gradually exposing them over time and letting them become hard, in the same way as with the exposed root style.

Growing-on-a-Rock Style or "Seki-joju"

On rocky terrains, trees are forced to search through cracks and holes with their roots for nutrient-rich soil. The roots are not protected before they reach the soil; therefore, they must shield themselves from the sun by growing a special bark around them. In bonsai, the root grows over a rock into the pot. Caring for this tree isn't exactly different from how you care for another style. Juniper and ficus bonsai are suitable for this style.

Double-Trunk Style or "Sokan"

Double-trunk style, as the name implies, represents a tree with two trunks. The trunks are usually from two trees of different lengths that grew together at the bottom, and the two trees are molded as one. No branches are allowed to come up between these trunks.

Clump Style

Whenever a fruit or a cone containing a lot of seeds fall onto a fertile soil and several trees grow at once, they may aggregate to form a tree with a number of trunks. Each trunk naturally curves outward from the bunch and grows upward in the direction of the light. The clump style in bonsai is designed by planting a number of seedlings closely together and modeling them so as to form outward-reaching trunks.

Raft Style or "Ikadabuki"

Under natural conditions, this style mimics a woodland tree destroyed by a strong wind that broke its branches on the lower side. After a long period, roots grow out of the trunk resting on the soil, and the rest of the branches (rising upward from the unaffected part of the trunk) will grow to give an appearance of a fresh tree connected by an old trunk. In bonsai, a one-sided tree is wounded with wires and laid flat on the soil. Making a cut on the bark will expose the cambium-containing layer beneath the trunk. Sprinkle rooting powder on it. That way, the growth of the roots will be enhanced. A vertical trunk normally forms a straight line of trees. Using a bent trunk will add a more fascinating style of trees that will look like a small grove.

Forest Style or "Yose-ue"

By combining five or more trees, an artist can design a bonsai that looks like a miniature forest. Sometimes the forest is made in such a way that it looks as if it reaches far into the distance. If shorter trees were planted in front and larger ones behind, it will give a far-view perception. An alternative perspective is that of a viewer in the midst of the trees viewing the forest, extending beyond. This is made by arranging the larger plants in the front. In both cases, trees of different diameters and heights should be used and planted, such that no three trees are arranged in a straight line when observed from the side or the front. The trees are all arranged apart from each other. The entire effect is a canopy that looks like a scalene triangle.

Weeping Style

Naturally, weeping trees are similar to willows in that they are often found in damp areas and along rivers, lakes, and streams. Bonsai artists try as much as possible to recreate this view by the meticulous use of wire to prime a tree, like a weeping cherry or willow. In order to make the form in a miniature version, each branch should be wired, such that it curves upward and then forms a sharp, downward bend to mimic the weep.

Shari Bonsai Style ("Sharimiki")

As time passes, some trees start to develop bark-less or bald places on their trunks due to harsh weather conditions. This bald portion usually starts at the point where the roots emanate from the soil and grow thinner as it goes up the trunk. High sunlight will bleach these areas to form a characteristic portion of the tree. For bonsai, these areas are debarked with a sharp knife and treated with calcium sulfate so as to hasten the bleaching process.

Chapter 3

Types of Bonsai

There are vast varieties of trees one can choose from to create bonsai. To make the best choice, certain factors must be considered, such as where you reside, the amount of time you wish to spend caring for the tree, and the kind of space available. All of these factors will determine which style of bonsai will be best for you. An inexperienced person can also learn this art relatively easily by practicing and implementing tested and approved techniques in this book. Listed below are a few types.

Japanese Maple. The Japanese maple blossoms under shade, and it is well known for its fragile leaves that transform into a beautiful shade of yellow, orange, or red. It is easy to mold in any desired form, but it is recommended to do all pruning and styling in spring.

Azalea. Azalea is the most popular and easiest form of bonsai, especially for starters. The azalea has beautiful petals that reflect its beauty. However, it must not be placed under direct sunlight and must be nourished with adequate fertilizers before it begins to blossom.

Fukien Tea. This is a very minute genus of tropical tree that ought to be placed in the full rays of direct sunlight for not more than sixty minutes. Due to the tiny nature of the shoots, an artist can easily wire new shoots to mold the tree. The pots should be changed every two to three years, in early spring. Two species are used mostly. Both are woody, branch easily, have small and glossy leaves, and bloom periodically all year round. The species with smaller leaves develops its trunk slowly but have tiny red fruit prolifically.

Pomegranate. The pomegranate can be a colorful addition to your bonsai collection with its red trumpet-shaped flowers, tiny bright-green leaves, and tiny round orange-red ornamental fruit. This makes it one of the most preferred deciduous bonsais.

Magnolia. This is mainly a very slow-growing shrub that can be planted as a bonsai. This plant teaches patience because it will take between twenty-five to thirty years before it bears flowers. The flowers are white in color and star-shaped. Without leaves, the magnolia flowers look fascinating on the bonsai.

Flowering Crabapple. Any apple species would make a beautiful bonsai. However, the flowering crabapple overshadows the rest when it comes to complete beauty. One may try out various styles on crabapples as well, though the upright formal type is the most preferable. The tree bears small green-red sour apples, with either pink, red, or white petals. This is highly recommended for amateurs.

Bougainvillea. Bougainvillea is a versatile shrub, with its multicolored flowers and bright-green leaves. It is one of the most common bonsais found in most plant nurseries. This can be styled in a cascading manner and is one of the few bonsai trees that love full exposure to the sun. They are easy to take care of and are fast growers.

Juniper. This is likely the most recognized of bonsai tree types. *The Karate Kid* bonsai made it quite popular. The plant itself often looks like a tree and can easily give the appearance of nature despite its small size.

Bamboo Bonsai. Difficult but beautiful.

Buttonwood. There are various kinds of bonsai trees that could be found in the tropics. A good example is the *Conocarpus erectus* found naturally in the Florida Keys and is one of the commonly used trees.

Boxwood Bonsai. This is an evergreen shrub, with broadleaf and hardwood, good for carving.

Black olive Bonsai. Scientifically, black olives are the dwarf version of *Bucida spinosa* and are not created from "black olives." It is popular due to its random growth pattern.

The Brazilian Rain Tree. This is a tree that is found naturally in the tropics, such as those in Brazil. It thrives well indoors.

Chrysanthemum Bonsai. This is not rare in Western culture due to a number of reasons. But certain bonsai enthusiasts, such as John Capobianco and Dale Cochoy, loved them.

Chinese Elm. Many amateurs, as well as other bonsai growers everywhere, prefer the Chinese elms. This is because they are easy to care for. Also, different styles can be created through pruning, with less effort.

Ficus. This is also known as figs. It is one of the most common plants used for indoor bonsai. They are good for shaping canopy-style bonsai and can be found in all tropical regions around the world. (There are over one hundred species worldwide).

Bald Cypress (*Taxodium distichum*). This bonsai is very popular in the southeastern regions of the U.S., where it grows naturally in the wild.

Carissa Bonsai. Popularly known as "natal plum," it is a tropical tree that is found by nature in Africa. It blossoms indoors when exposed to a sufficient amount of light. At times, it blooms with some fruit when grown outdoors.

Hornbeam. Although the hornbeam has many species, only a few are used to make amazing bonsai. One of the reasons is due to the fall color!

Jaboticaba. This is a graceful, fruit-bearing bonsai tree believed to do better indoors. Exotic fruit and flowers can be found growing naturally on the trunk and heavy branches.

Jade Bonsai. *Portulacaria afra* has shorter internodes and much smaller leaves. It is also much easier to nurture as a fine bonsai tree than the "common" jade plant, *Crassula argentea*.

Serissa Bonsai. Although serissa is an adorable tree to grow as a bonsai, it is difficult to grow.

Schefflera arboricola. This is a favorite tropical choice if you want an indoor bonsai tree. It is mostly preferred by beginners because it doesn't die off easily.

Sea Grape Bonsai. These are plants with large foliage. At first, they may be viewed as a rare type.

Tropical Mimosa Bonsai. This is obtained from *Leucaena glauca*. They can be planted as they grow easily and quickly from seed. (This is different from the temperate Albizzia.)

Mimosa Albizia. It is also called the silk tree and has pink flowers. Scientifically speaking, it is not related to the tropical mimosa.

Tamarind. It can withstand extensive root manipulation, wiring, heavy pruning, and even neglect for a short period. It is a tropical fruit tree.

Pine Tree Bonsai. This has wide varieties to choose from.

Powder Puff. This is one of the most recommended for indoor-blooming.

Pyracantha. Its berries can be orange, yellow, or red.

Bahama Berry. It is a special plant, native to the Bahamas.

Olive Bonsai. This is the native European "real" olive.

Water Jasmine (Wrightia). It is a heavy-blooming tropical bonsai.

Others include dwarf juniper, jade, bamboo, cypress, cherry trees, white pine, ginkgo, boxwood, etc. As you may have observed, the list is endless. Thus, one could create new beauties yearly and continue increasing the current collection.

Chapter 4

Selecting a Bonsai Tree

Bonsai trees are nurtured in a container or pot and primed into a desired shape or form. There are several types of bonsai that can be grown indoors. Although most individuals select a bonsai tree based on how beautiful it appears, it is imperative that you choose the right bonsai for the surroundings it will be grown in.

No matter what you desire, maybe to buy a bonsai tree, grow bonsai as an amateur, or begin with pre-bonsai, the following fundamental points will assist you to make a wise choice:

Size

There are no strict rules with respect to the definitive sizing in bonsai. However, most can be grouped as *small* (easy to lift and carried on one hand), *medium-sized* (requires both hands to lift up and hold), and *big* (requires more hands). It is therefore very imperative to choose wisely because, if things go well, you have to live together till the end. The tree might live longer than you! Moving a big bonsai tree is easy for young people. However, think about how difficult it will be when you grow older. Instead, if you choose a bonsai tree that is sized such that it fits in the palm of one hand, just forget about going for summer vacations unless you can find a trusted companion to help you care for your tree by watering it while you are away. For instance, some bonsai trees such as Mame are quite small and can grow up to four inches (ten centimeters). As an alternative, the Chinese elm bonsai tree (*Ulmus parviflora*) can be used to fill a bigger space, and it will look very good.

The Surroundings Where It Will be placed

Some require more specific environmental condition, such as indoor bonsai trees that need lights and protection from snow, and this should be considered when buying one. Some of the common conditions are listed below:

- In a room that gets really warm: *Carmona microphylla* (Oriental tea bonsai tree)

- Access to the sun in the morning and the evening: *Ulmus parviflora* (Chinese elm bonsai)

- Well-lit environment but not in direct contact with sunlight: *Ficus retusa* (Fig bonsai tree)

- Regular watering not important: *Crassulaovata* (Jade bonsai tree)

- Position with lots of bright light: *Sageretia theezans* (Chinese sweet plum bonsai tree) and *Crassula ovata* (Jade bonsai tree)

Grower's Experience

Based on the type of bonsai tree, some are more challenging to grow than others. If you are an amateur, lacking experience in growing bonsai, varieties, such as a dwarf Hawaiian umbrella bonsai tree (*Schefflera arboricola*), fig bonsai tree (*Ficus retusa*), and juniper (*Juniperus*) are quite common. They can survive in a wide range of climates and don't require strict care regime to survive. The thousand stars tree can also be used as well if you want something more intriguing.

Buying a Healthy Tree

The basic fact about growing a healthy tree is simply buying a healthy one. Here are what to watch out for when buying the tree to decide if it is a good and healthy bonsai tree.

- **Leaves.** The foliage on a bonsai ought to be a bright and healthy green color. None of the leaves should be dried out, pale, or discolored.

- **Branches.** A healthy bonsai must not have crossing branches, and the branches should not have even distribution throughout the shape of the tree.

- **Trunk.** It must be thicker at the base than at the top. The outer layer of the trunk is expected to be smooth.

- **Roots.** The roots should extend slightly out of the soil but should be carefully placed inside the pot.

Structural Features

Healthy Plant: This may seem easy to observe, but often, we find sickly plants that are beautifully shaped. At times, we may wish to save them! We need to avoid this temptation. Buy only trees that are healthy. Search for those with fresh green leaves or needles (depending upon the time of year), stable pots, and those free from pests. A yellow-green plant that is wobbly in the pot and/or misshapen or damaged leaves are all pointers of potential problems.

Trunk: Appearance of age is more important than actual age. Whether the tree is short or tall, if the trunk is a heavy trunk, the tree will appear older.

Taper: This means a trunk that is narrow toward the top and widest at the bottom. Branches are also expected to be narrow toward the tip. Trunks and/or branches with pole shape will rarely become good bonsai.

Proportion: Leaves, flowers, and fruit must be in line with the entire size of your bonsai. If you wish to buy a bonsai tree that will have a small size, large leaves and flowers will make it look more like a shrub or bush rather than a tree.

Scars and dead branches often can be used to tell the age of a tree. If you find a tree with scars on it, you already have a good start.

Nebari: *Nebari* is a Japanese word that means surface roots that spread away from the foot of the tree trunk. That flare is highly cherished and contributes to the look of age.

Foremost Branch: If you wish to purchase a bonsai that is an upright plant, a healthy first branch is imperative. That first branch is about one-third of the way up the tree. It is also expected to be heavier than the other branches of the tree. If part of the large branches is at the top of a plant, go for another plant. This "first-branch" principle may not apply to all styles, such as literati or *bunjin* style.

Before paying for a bonsai tree, avoid the misleading assumptions!

- Keep in mind that a small bonsai in a small pot will never grow to become a large bonsai. One of the reasons for keeping it in a small pot is to keep it small. The saying that bigger is better is not always true.

- The fact that a particular plant is well known as bonsai—for instance, the juniper—does not mean all will make a good bonsai tree for you!

Bonsai Material

Bonsai lovers of our days do not realize and appreciate what they now enjoy. Back in the days, searching for bonsai material such as shrubs, trees, and plants trained into bonsai was very difficult. But these days, one can find bonsai material and potted trees in horticultural stores, garden, hardware stores, mall, kiosks, and online stores. The best place to get plant material options is garden centers and online stores. Floral stores, mall, and kiosks often have expensive collections of potted trees.

Outdoor or Indoor Bonsai Tree?

The most commercially available and most commonly grown bonsai trees are the serissa, fukien tea, ficus, and the juniper. Bonsai enthusiasts may argue that there is no such thing as an indoor bonsai, and in a way, they would be right. A bedroom, house, or apartment is not the natural environment for any tree. But with time, a plant can get used to the indoor environment over the winter and stay healthy enough to survive until summer and spring before it is taken back outdoors.

If you decide to pick a juniper as your bonsai, be ready to care for it during winter, as it possibly dries out in the house because of the dry air, which is observed in most homes during winter. And if you abandon it to the elements outdoors, it will freeze and die unless it is maintained under the appropriate temperature. Choose a bonsai that is best for you. If you own a home with a garage, where you can winter your trees, choose hardy evergreens and deciduous shrubs and trees as your bonsai specimen. If you live in an apartment, choose a tree from one of the tropical plants.

Growing bonsai can bring as many benefits as any other niche in gardening. What you desire when selecting a bonsai will depend on your reply to a few questions:

- **What size of bonsai tree do you desire?** If you live in an apartment with a small balcony, having a large bonsai will be unreasonable. Choose a smaller bonsai tree that is easy to display and protect from bad weather.

- **How much are you willing to spend on a bonsai tree?** You may buy bonsai in various stages of development and quality, ranging from forty to one thousand dollars.

- **Is there enough space suitable to properly winter an outdoor bonsai tree?** If there isn't enough space, you ought to think about a tropical tree that can survive the winter when kept indoors.

Chapter 5

The Vital Tools

Most amateurs who wish to learn the art of bonsai are often confused with respect to the type of tools needed to aid them in learning the bonsai skills. The right tools are very imperative for the care and nurturing of bonsai trees. You must be able to cut accurately on the trees, with clean and even edges.

For learners, it is suggested to get a few fundamental tools as a start, such as a good concave cutter and a quality shear. Along the line, when you've made some progress, you will need more intensive tools to work on your bonsai.

One of the most suggested, high-quality tools are the Japanese bonsai tools, which are well known for their high quality (though expensive), but Chinese tools provide much better quality for their prices. The metal ore (black steel), from which most tools are formed, requires a bit more maintenance because it may rust. High-quality stainless-steel tools are even more expensive. It is very important to apply the tools properly and handle them with care.

That way, they will last for a long time.

Shears and Pliers

There are shears of various sizes and shapes. They are useful in cutting twigs, smaller branches, foliage, or roots.

If the majority of the trees in your collection are small bonsai, you don't need to purchase large shears and pliers! There are strong shears with a wide, standard shape strong enough for stronger twigs and shears with narrower and longer shapes that can be used for a dense canopy while smaller shears can be used for trimming azaleas or *shohin* bonsai and removing their wilted flowers.

There are concave cutters with partially curved blades, those with straight blades, and knob cutters, which can be used to create deep cuts. Concave cutters can be used to cut branches from a trunk, especially when you desire to make deeps cuts that will heal with no trace nor scar. These various pliers are available in different sizes:

- Knob cutter
- Tweezers spatula
- Large foldable saw
- Pruning shear
- Root hook
- Small root rake
- Medium-sized foldable saw
- Thin pruning saw
- Grafting knife with a wooden sheath
- Standard shear
- Long, slim twig shear
- Leaf-cutter
- Jin/wire-bending plier

- Large wire cutter
- Small wire cutter
- Sickle knife
- Root plier
- Strong, standard shear for root pruning
- Small-angled jin/wire-bending plier
- Set of soil scoops
- *Shohin* and azalea shear
- Large, concave cutter with straight blades
- Small concave cutter with straight blades
- Larger root rake
- Sickle saw

Knives and Saws

Saws are needed when you need to cut branches, trunks, or roots, which are too hard or too thick for pliers to cut. Remember that Japanese pruning saws will make a cut when you pull them back toward yourself. Therefore, avoid pushing them strongly to prevent the blade from bending or breaking. If you wish to smoothen the cuts and wounds caused by pliers and saws, grafting knives are the most appropriate tool. They are similar to knives used by skilled gardeners.

Tools for Roots and Repotting

Removing root-ball from the pot requires special sickle saw and sickle knives that can be used for cutting along the inside of the pot. Thick, angular, plastic bowls that will allow you to work on the roots or mix new soil will make work much easier and neater. Root rakes and root hooks are available in various sizes, with one to three teeth, and can be used for opening up the root-ball, carefully combing the roots and extracting old soil that is stuck to the roots.

Root pruning can be carried out by using a strong, standard shear with big, solid blades and strong holders. If you encounter a stubborn root, use pliers or a saw.

Assuming you wish to use a sandy soil, such as *kanuma, akadama,* pumice, etc., you need to sieve the soil before you use it to separate the dust particles. In practice, there are sieves of various sizes that are made of stainless steel. These sieves are of different mesh sizes. Scoops are available for filling the soil into the bonsai pot, and they are of different sizes, which are specifically designed for adding soil under the roots. If you wish to move the soil further into cavities between the roots of the bonsai, bamboo sticks or chopsticks are very useful. But you need to exercise great caution in order not to damage the roots by stabbing them too hard. For adding moss or uprooting weeds, you need a tweezers spatula, which performs a double function of pressing wet moss to the soil and for removing stubborn weeds.

Tools for Wiring

Making a bonsai usually requires the use of wires to position and shape branches and trunk. Aluminum or annealed copper wire may be used for this purpose. The wire cutters which are sold at local hardware stores are good enough for cutting wire when applying it to bonsai. Most often, it is recommended to remove training wires by cutting them off. The training wire is in direct contact with the limb or trunk. Thus, only the edge of the wire cutter is used to cut the wire. Else, the branch may be severely damaged.

The relatively long cutting blades sold at hardware stores have very few mechanical advantages at the tips, making wire removal a challenging activity. Individuals with physical ailments, such as arthritis, may find wire removal quite difficult while using standard wire cutters. Therefore, bonsai wire cutters use very short cutting blades. This greatly enhances the mechanical benefits of the tool.

For wiring a bonsai tree, you definitely need wires with various diameters, a wire cutter, and pliers for annealing the wire, which is also useful for deadwood *(jin)*. Those tools are of different shapes and sizes. Purchase small ones if you have plenty of *shohin* bonsai. Wires made from annealed copper or aluminum are made specifically for bonsai. Amateurs need to use aluminum as it is easier to use.

Tools for Bending (and Protective Materials)

If you wish to bend trunks or branches very heavily, protective measures are necessary to avoid breaking the wood and tearing the bark. It also aids the healing process of minor cracks and fissures without causing the death of the branch or trunk. The traditional technique is to bind wet raffia tightly around the portion you wish to bend before the wire is applied. Binding tape made of rubber (wounded around or on top of a gauze) or tubes from bicycle tires can also be used for this purpose.

For heavy bending, there are tools, like specially designed massive steel levers, cushioned with rubber. Special screw clamps of different sizes and shapes can be used. Turnbuckles are important as they can be used for tightening strong guy wires at regular intervals. Iron rebar is useful as a lever for bending strong branches, and you can also use wood-wedges and guy wires for wiring. Thin, transparent tubes, such as those found in fish tanks or infusion hoses, can be used for protecting the trunks, branches, and roots before wrapping the wire around it.

Tools and Carving Knives for Deadwood

The primary aim of working on deadwood is to ensure it appears natural and free from traces of human intervention. It seems fascinating that a wide variety of tools are available for this purpose.

A slim, blunt chisel is ideal for lifting wood fibers. Various loop knives and carving hooks can be used for carving slight furrows and for peeling off bark, and it should follow the course of the fibers.

The branch splitters, on the other hand, are sharp pliers used for splitting dead stumps and branches. For breaking small wood (less fibrous wood) or for splitting fibers (on conifers with fibrous wood), the *jin* plier is a recommended tool.

There are a number of variously shaped carving tools, often sold together, in different sizes and qualities, which are useful for smoothing, contouring, shaping, narrowing, or hollowing out the deadwood.

In a bid to wipe out every last trace of your work and remove wood fibers that are sticking out, it is advisable to apply a gas torch, which is fueled with methane gas, for instance. After burning, the charred wood layer can be brushed off with brass, steel, or nylon brushes.

For conserving decaying or decayed deadwood, wood hardener can be applied. They can be made from liquid plastics, mixed in acetone. The common Japanese *jin* fluid is made of lime sulfur, often used for whitening the deadwood and preserving it.

Other Bonsai Tools

Below are tools for wiring, bending, carving, and repotting bonsai:

- Raffia

- Gun oil
- Camellia oil
- Fusing rubber tape and gauze
- Infusion hose
- Brass brush
- Steel brush
- Toothbrush
- Coco brush
- Branch/Trunk-bending lever
- Screw clamp
- Rust eraser (dark grey) and grindstone
- Disinfectant
- Nylon brush
- Bicycle tube

Electronic Bonsai Tools

When electrically powered tools are used, great caution is required to avoid injuries, which may occur quite easily. The use of protective glasses is recommended to avoid wood splinters or metal bristles from getting hurled into your eyes. Also, gloves, dust mask, and even a helmet are all necessary for extensive deadwood work when using powerful electric bonsai to avoid distractions while working. Full concentration and thoughtfulness are required. Also, hold on to the machine firmly with your hands, and be cautious with the speed controller dial and the on/off switch.

Makita has bits with a six-millimeter shank and is one of the most commonly used large machines among bonsai enthusiasts although other manufacturers produce similar machines. It is imperative for you to pick a machine with a speed control button because different woods require different speed. There is a variety of powerful tools, like cutting wheels, circular saws, rotating brushes made of different materials, grinding bits, and abrasive wheels in many different shapes. Because of the huge power and weight of the large grinder machines, this often makes their use dangerous and difficult. They are not advisable for learners and amateurs.

Dremel, however, is a smaller machine for which a huge variety of bits of a three-millimeter shank are available. There are other machines similar to this produced by other manufacturers, for which the same bits can be applied, like rotating brushes made of nylon, steel or brass for extracting bark and smoothening deadwood, various grinders, cutters, abrasive wheels, and many more.

Some bonsai enthusiasts make use of sandblasting equipment for deadwood work. Those are large, costly devices, for which protective gear, an ideal work environment, and special technical knowledge are required. The deadwood work method often gives fascinating results.

Electronic bonsai tools used for carving and working on deadwood include the following:

- Branch splitter
- Spear plough
- Small loop knife
- Strong, straight scalpel
- Gas torch
- Protective glasses
- Dremel 300 machine
- Curved scalpel
- A set of ten small carving tools
- A collection of circular brushes, grinders, and screw wrenches for large grinders
- *Jin* liquid

- Makita GD800C die grinder
- Wood hardener
- A collection of important Dremel tools (grinders, circular brushes, screw wrench, abrasive wheels, and drill-bits)
- A set of four flex-cut carving tools
- A set of five different carving tools
- Round carving hook, with a thin, sharp tip
- Small, angled *jin* plier
- Angled carving hook
- Large *jin* pliers

Materials and Tools for Maintenance

Rust erasers can be used for removing rust and dirt on the tools' blades. For honing the blades, various types of grindstones are available in the market. Bonsai tools should be decontaminated regularly. This is necessary to prevent bacteria or virus infections and growth of fungi from spreading from one tree to another. To maintain hinges and blades, gun oil or camellia oil can be used. Coco brushes are useful for sweeping *nebaris*, soil surfaces, trunks, shelves, tables, tools, and so on.

Watering Tools and Systems

There are different shapes and sizes of watering cans. For watering a small collection of bonsai trees, a ball-shower or a watering can could be used, but it must have a long neck and a fine nozzle to produce enough pressure to force the water out of the tiny holes of the nozzle. However, a garden hose with a sprinkler could be used if you have a large bonsai collection.

For sprinkling the bonsai trees with water, leaf fertilizer solution, or plant protection products, you need spray cans. Either those with a manual pump which you must pump with your fingers for each spray puff or those you have to pump before use.

An automated bonsai watering system is available for those who cannot water their trees properly when they are at work or when they are on vacation. This will help out for a few days. You can have a time-operated lawn sprinkler in front of your trees.

Though there are more complex and reliable watering systems (such as Tropf-Blumat, Gardena MDS, misting systems, and flooding systems), they are quite expensive. However, they are worth the expense. Get enough information about each one if you are interested.

In many areas, the tap water contains a lot of chlorine, which makes the water unfit for bonsai trees, such as azaleas and maples, which require soft water. Well, water is also rich in calcium and iron. Therefore, collecting rainwater is necessary. A rain pipe channeled to a barrel, channeled in a downward manner or a larger water tank will work effectively, as well as a large, underground water tank or cistern, from which you can obtain the water, with an electrical pump or hand-operated pump.

Turntables

Bonsai tree care can be easier when done on turntables, which have simple, flat, rotary discs. Massive turntables, which can be slanted in different directions, or vertically adjustable turntables on three legs are most convenient rather than using ordinary tables that require lifting the pot every now and then.

Bonsai Turntables

- Three-legged turntable with adjustable height

- Simple flat wooden rotary disc
- Wooden turntable, which can be tilted in two directions

Tool Maintenance

Normally, bonsai tools ought to be cleaned and oiled after every use. Turpentine can be used for removing sap on the blades. After you're done cleaning, the tool should be wiped dry with an oily rag, paying special attention to the cutting edges of the blades. Be cautious because the blades are very sharp and dangerous.

It is necessary to perform this important task after any use that exposes the tools to large amounts of moisture, sap, or perspiration. Tools which are exposed to temperature and humidity variations on storage will corrode very fast due to condensation of moisture.

What to Buy

A complete collection of bonsai tools is not compulsory for beginners. Commence with a concave pruner and maybe a pair of bud shears. Buy other tools as your expertise and requirements increase. When you are convinced that you have more than mere interest in bonsai, knob cutters, wire cutters, a root hook, and root pruners should be purchased.

There is a vast range of quality and prices of bonsai tools. What to buy is a personal decision, but I will suggest you go for Japanese products because any Japanese bonsai tools, even those with poor quality, are more superior to those made in other countries. A lot of Japanese companies are involved in the production of various bonsai tools. The best are prohibitively expensive, even for bonsai enthusiasts.

The nature of the style of bonsai also determines the tools that will be used. For instance, outdoor tools, unlike fine woodworking tools, are exposed to a substantial amount of moisture, corrosive perspiration, and the risk of getting lost. If it is misplaced for only one or two days, the outdoor environment is likely to destroy the working surfaces of the tool that is exposed to the weather. Bonsai tools that are plated with an anticorrosive layer or those made of stainless steel are best purchased for outdoor bonsai. Silver-plated tools are found to be resistant to rust. Sadly, silver-coated tools are not as sharp as those made of steel and are twice or thrice as expensive.

If you use bonsai tools properly, the cutting edges will last for a long time, without the need for honing. Corrosion and improper use will definitely degrade cutting potential of a bonsai tool. Knob cutters, concave cutters, and root cutters have quite a complex blade conformation, which makes efficient sharpening difficult for most bonsai enthusiasts and even professional sharpeners as well. Apart from the bud scissors, sharpened bonsai tools rarely function as much as new ones. Thus, try as much as possible to limit spending so much sharpening the tools by purchasing the latest expensive grade of Japanese tool, but go for those that fall within your budget.

Chapter 6

Cultivation

You ought to consider that there are numerous ways to grow a bonsai before asking yourself how to do it. You could begin from zero, which implies purchasing seeds from a store or picking the seeds up close to the trees around your house or in the wild. You can likewise find or purchase a "pre-bonsai," a young plant, which is comprised of a germinated tree in an early stage. The entire procedure turns out to be quicker that way. Remember though that growing a bonsai is also an exercise of patience. The last option might be the least educational but also the least difficult—that is, to purchase a bonsai that is fully grown. You would only need to do caring activities in that case.

It's crucial to know "bonsai seeds" do not exist. If you are offered such a product by someone, he's either being a liar or doesn't know much about bonsai. A regular tree seed is a seed from which a bonsai originates. The process of making a bonsai follows later after germination has occurred.

Bonsai Soil

Numerous different soil mixtures utilized in planting bonsai exists. Bonsai individuals in Florida, Japan, Scotland, Holland, Canada, and California all have diverse conditions for growth and varying materials available to make soil mixtures. Most mixtures don't utilize garden soil—one thing they have in common. This is due to the fact that shallow pots don't drain as excellently as the soil in the garden does, and the roots can remain excessively wet and rot as a result!

Soil pH

Soil pH is a measure of the soil's acidity or alkalinity on a zero to fourteen scale. Neutral is seven, while under seven is acidic, and greater than seven is alkali. Soil pH influences the measure of nutrients that are soluble in soil water and, therefore, the measure of nutrient available to plants. While some nutrients are more available under acid conditions, other nutrients are more available under alkaline conditions. Nearly neutral soil, 6.5 pH, is preferred by most deciduous trees (for instance, maples and elms). But a slightly more acidic soil, around 5.5 pH, is preferred by conifers.

- For moisture retention, *akadama* and sand are utilized. *Akadama* is also slightly acidic.

- To improve drainage, lava and pumice are utilized. Lava possesses an average porosity of 70–90 percent, dependent a bit on size and type, and is listed as an inert material, so no effect on values of pH.

- Pumice has a tendency to increase pH values slightly and has an average porosity of 90 percent. It has the additional advantage of weighing considerably less than lava. Using *kanume* (4.5–5 pH) in place of pumice is recommended for pines and junipers. They prefer soil that is slightly more acidic.

- Turface is most generally utilized as a soil additive to aid in drainage improvement. While soil compaction is being decreased, Turface absorbs its weight in water, which is what you need from bonsai soil. So it acts like *akadama* or *kanume* in that regard and is a lot more affordable. Numerous individuals use Turface successfully in place of *akadama*.

Soil Size

The size of the particles utilized is vital. For instance, you'll find that more than a mixture made utilizing smaller particles, a mixture made using bigger particles will drain more quickly. A small pot will contain less soil and has the tendency to dry out more quickly than a bigger pot. By making use of smaller-sized soil particles in the mix, we can protect a small pot from drying out too rapidly.

The table below shows the particle size recommended for various size pots.

Pot Size	Particle Size
Deep	(> 3" deep) 1/2"
Medium	(1.5" to 3" deep) 3/8"
Shallow	(<1.5" deep) 1/4"
Shohin	(e.g., 4" diameter) 1/8"

To make soil mixture, the different materials are sorted first (see tables below) into the appropriate size and then combined. A sieve

BONSAI

is usually used for sorting. Typically, sieves are made with three screens that enable you to sort your materials into the appropriate size, according to the table above.

Making Soil

Here's how to make a "soil mix." Each material will be sifted thrice. First, using the biggest screen, sift and put the material that doesn't fall through the screen into one heap or bucket. Now, sift the material that went through the biggest screen, again, using the medium screen. Put the material that doesn't fall through the screen into a separate heap or bucket. Now, sift again using the finest screen and put the material that doesn't fall through the screen into a third heap or bucket. Just very small particles or dust will pass through this screen. This dust should be disposed of or kept to make muck (as described below).

Combine each component in the ratios shown in the table below, now that you have them sorted into three different sizes

Material	Ratio
Pumice	1
Red-and-black Lava	2
Calcined Clay	1
Pine Bark	1
Expanded Slate	1

Putting Soil in the Pot

You will generally place a layer of soil that is shallow in the base of the pot. Place your bonsai in the pot and add similar-sized soil above the roots. It appears to be of value to use a layer of larger soil at the base to enable the soil to drain faster, particularly when pots are deeper than three inches.

Replacing the top soil once or twice each year is recommended. It eliminates salt build-up and unwanted plants. Gently rake the surface over the edge using a chopstick or small rake. Be mindful of the roots to avoid damage. After this, place fresh soil on top and settle it in around the roots using a chopstick.

Muck

Muck is another vital "soil" mixture. It is a paste, and it's used as a binding agent to hold soil or objects, such as rocks, stable inside the pot until the tree roots are established. Muck is frequently used to make an edge that will guard against the soil mixture sliding off, when a rock slab, such as slate, is used in place of a pot. To do this, roll muck between your two hands until it appears like a rope, maybe with a diameter of one-half inch. After this, lay out the rope on top of the rock slab and arrange it until you are satisfied with the shape. Usually, its shape should be irregular. Press it down after this until it adheres to the rock slab. You can now add your trees and soil mixture.

Recipe: Sift the adobe soil, keeping just the fines (dust to one-eighth inch). A screen that's of similar size to a window screen, or slightly smaller, should be used. Some peat moss can be long and stringy. If yours fit this description, cut it into lengths, approximately two inches long, using scissors. Mix half-adobe and half-peat moss after this. Add enough water simply needed for it to be kneaded to a dough-like consistency. If you place the mixture into a heavy-duty zip lock bag, it's not difficult to knead.

Hint: You can get black adobe that will make the best-looking muck, but it's hard to get. Actually, contingent on where you live, any type of adobe soil may be hard to find. You are most likely discarding the dust when you sift if you are making use of *akadama* in your soil mix. Don't do that. Instead, make use of it in this recipe.

Storage: Store any leftover you have in the ziplock bag in your freezer. (Yes, in your freezer. This will prevent it from turning moldy.) Simply remove it from the freezer, let it defrost, add a little more water if necessary, and knead it a bit afterward to make it flexible and ready for use when you need it for your next project.

This soil recipe works in microclimates, especially those that exist around Orlando, Florida. You'll have to slightly modify the mix if your weather is warmer or cooler than those kinds of microclimates.

Bonsai Cultivation Techniques

Growing Bonsai from Seed

(In Japanese, *misho*) Growing Bonsai from tree seeds gives you total control from the earliest stage possible, and it can be extremely rewarding. This is the only way a Bonsai can be grown right from the start although it takes a long time (not less than three years) before you have a tree you can begin working on.

To start with, seeds need to be acquired. You can decide to purchase them in an (online) store, or you can collect them from trees in your environment. Always remember that things such as "special bonsai tree seeds" do not exist, as bonsai are made from normal trees.

Planting the seeds in autumn will be just fine if you collected them from trees growing in your surroundings. However, if you plan to plant the seeds out of season (during springtime, for instance), buy seeds online, or have a preference for seedlings from trees not growing in your surroundings, it might be necessary to go through a process referred to as "stratification."

Stratification

To maximize the time frame of their first growth season, many tree-species have their seeds genetically programmed to survive all through winter and germinate in early spring. Actually, a large amount of these seeds won't be able to grow until after a cold period. So it may be important to make a mimicry of the cold season by storing the seeds at a cold spot for a few weeks if you want to plant seeds for bonsai. This increases the rate of germination significantly.

Most tree species will need to have their seeds soaked in water first and then put away in your fridge for a couple of months. The appropriate measure of time and the ideal temperature is dependent on the tree species. A quick online search will furnish you with a correct answer. This might be somewhat complicated for beginners. It is, therefore, advisable to gather seeds from tree species found close to you, place the seeds outside, and plant them in early spring, the same way Mother Nature does!

Where?

You can collect seeds from trees growing in your surroundings in autumn, as mentioned before. Seeds, such as chestnuts and acorns, are not difficult to obtain in the forest. Conifer seeds can be found inside pinecones. You have to store the pinecones in a warm place, so they will discharge the seeds from between the scales after you collect them. Bonsai shops (online) also have seeds of various tree species available for purchase.

When?

Autumn is the best time to sow seeds. This enables you to follow

BONSAI

nature's time plan, and the young seedling will have a full summer to develop after germination has taken place early spring. This also implies that you don't have to worry about stratification.

From Seedling to Bonsai

Let us examine the developmental stages of seedlings first before we begin to propagate trees from seed. Growing bonsai from seed is an incredible way to style bonsai trees without having to prune thick branches (which is frequently inherent to styling *yamadori* or nursery stock), but it will be a test of your patience.

Growing Bonsai from Seed, Step by Step

1. First, a layer of a coarse, water-draining substrate, similar to lava rock or grit, should be applied
2. Add a layer of standard bonsai soil after this.
3. Buy or collect tree seeds and check them out to determine if they require scarification or stratification. That is mostly dependent on the tree species you choose to grow.
4. Put the seeds on the soil. Leave out some room between the seeds.
5. A top layer of standard bonsai soil should be added. About an inch (two centimeters) of it is sufficient.
6. Add the soil, and use your fingers to compact the soil a bit.
7. Lastly, water thoroughly. From now on, keep the seedbed slightly moist.

Pros of Growing from Seed

Due to the fact that you will be able to impact all the growth stages, this is most likely the best way to have complete control over your bonsai. Being involved in the beginning cycle of a tree can be exciting and fulfilling.

Cons

Some seeds will take months to germinate while some will not germinate if the conditions are not right for germination. It is a slow process. Secondly, it will take a longer time before they are ready to be trained, even if germination was successful. One advantage though, while your plants are growing, is that you have a great amount of time to learn more about the craft.

Things to Look Out For

Seeds that would normally germinate (in the wild) in the same season and climatic condition that you are planting are the easiest to germinate.

Conditions might not be optimum for seed germination sometimes. It may be because of the following reasons:

- Seeds have been in storage for a long time.
- Generally, that tree species does not grow in the climate/region they are being germinated in.
- Seeds have been planted out of season.

If this is the case, then the need to pre-treat the seeds may arise to encourage the seed to germinate, by exposing them to the conditions under which they would germinate in the wild. This procedure is referred to as stratification.

How to Care for Your Plant Once They Germinate

You will most likely begin by planting plenty of seeds. Each growth phase is a chance to dispose of the least healthy. For instance, it is likely that not all your seeds will germinate, and you can select the healthiest plants to keep from the seeds that do. After some time, you might select a few to wire and so on.

Put the seedlings in a sunny spot once they have sprouted, and let them be. It is not the ideal time to repot or prune. Additionally, they are not strong enough to withstand fertilizer yet. The seedlings can be repotted in the following spring.

Root Pruning

Seedlings will develop a root system comprising of both tap and fine roots that are more defined over time. Usually, trees develop long roots (tap roots) in the wild, which is strong enough to push into the soil, not just to provide stability for the tree but also to absorb nutrients from the soil. In addition, they develop finer roots that grow laterally. We prefer not to encourage these long roots in bonsai; rather, we encourage the better ones. To achieve this, a sharp knife is used to prune the taproot.

Making a Compact Tree

A compact tree starts with a compact root framework. It is, therefore, important to pay attention to your tree's root structure within the first year. After germination has taken place, it should be pruned within the first year. A lot of patience is required to grow bonsai from seed, but it is worth it. During the process, you'll learn one of the great lessons that anybody who has been involved in it for a while will tell you—how to have patience and enjoy the journey. Do not look forward to the destination alone.

Key Takeaway

It takes a great deal of time to grow trees from cuttings and wait for not less than three years without pruning. It is recommended to repot the seedlings after the first year into big pots.

BONSAI

Growing Bonsai from Cuttings

In Japanese: *sashiki*. Among bonsai growers, cultivating trees from cuttings is extremely common as it is a cost-effective way to propagate new trees. The time it takes to grow trees from seeds is reduced by about a year if this method is used while also giving you the advantage of knowing ahead of time the qualities that will be possessed by the cutting.

Appropriate cuttings have to be collected to begin with. Most tree types (specifically deciduous trees and a few conifers) are propagated easily using cuttings. Choose a branch of an existing tree and cut it off. The cuttings should be about two to four inches in size, five to ten centimeters tall, and have a thickness of two to five millimeters. It is also possible to take larger cuttings. However, there is a slim chance of getting them to root.

When?

In general, the ideal times to cut off and plant cuttings is in spring and summer. A few hardwood cuttings can be prepared and planted after their growth season (late summer).

Growing bonsai from seed is an incredible way to style bonsai trees without having to prune thick branches (which is frequently inherent to styling *yamadori* or nursery stock), but it will be a test of your patience.

Growing Bonsai from Seed, Step by Step

1. First, a layer of a coarse, water-draining substrate, similar to lava rock or grit, should be applied.

2. Add a layer of standard bonsai soil after this.

3. Prune a couple of branches from the tree to be used as cuttings.

4. Use a sharp twig shear to prune the branch at an angle of forty-five degrees.

5. Put the cuttings about one inch (two centimeters) in the soil.

6. Water thoroughly after this. Keep the soil slightly moist. The cuttings will begin to grow in a couple of weeks.

Key Takeaway

It is not difficult to grow trees from cutting. But before you can begin to shape them, it takes a couple of years. Be patient. Give the cuttings a chance to grow before you begin pruning and repotting.

Growing Bonsai from Nursery Stock / Pre-Bonsai

Young garden plants are referred to as nursery stocks (also known as pre-bonsai). They sometimes have great characteristics for bonsai purposes. A quick method of "propagating" a tree is by purchasing bonsai nursery stock, and you can start immediately with training it. It is a rather cheap and quick way to increase your bonsai collection although it can be difficult to obtain good material.

Commencing work on an older tree (rather than growing it right from the start) often means that you will need to remove large branches, with wounds that are visible, as a result, and this is a major drawback.

Where to Find Pre-Bonsai / Nursery Stock

It can be difficult to find good quality nursery stock. Try looking at some small family-owned nurseries (large business stores don't sell rough material often). Some (online) bonsai stores sell nursery stock also. This, however, comes at a price higher than prices at small nurseries.

When?

Nursery stock can be purchased all through the year, but most materials are available from early spring until late summer.

What to Look for in Nursery Stock

This is rather difficult to explain. Once you learn more about growing bonsai, your skills to discover potential materials will improve. Be that as it may, key aspects to look out for are the species of a bonsai tree, the trunk's shape, tapering of the trunk, the branching structure of the tree, and its *nebari* (root flare or surface roots).

And then?

The newly purchased nursery stock should be put outside (except it is an indoor tree) and kept moist but not wet. Normal quantities, as described in the chapter on fertilization, can be used to fertilize the trees. Whether you can begin training the tree immediately or not is dependent on the season in which you purchase the nursery stock. You can prune and repot trees immediately if purchased during the early spring, but you should wait until the next spring if you purchase trees later in the year.

Growing Bonsai from Collecting Trees (Yamadori)

(In Japanese: *yamadori*) Sometimes, due to natural circumstances, such as an absence of nutrients, trees that remained small can be found in nature. Although digging out the trees and transporting them home successfully can be difficult, these trees are the ones that often possess exceptional characteristics for bonsai purposes. Note that digging out plants from forests is likely illicit. Permission ought to be granted by the landowner.

BONSAI

When?

The ideal time to dig out bonsai trees is during the early spring for most bonsai tree species, just before the tree starts to grow.

Step-by-Step Plan for Collecting Trees from Forests

1. The initial step is to dig around the tree carefully with a spade. Take adequate care not to damage its root system.

2. Lift the tree carefully and place it on (possibly moisturized) sheets. Now to stop the tree from drying out, wrap the sheets around the tree's root system. Once you arrive back home, the tree should be potted as soon as you can.

3. Some of the original soil mixtures where the tree was dug out should be collected. It should be utilized to prepare a soil mixture for the tree.

4. A rather big pot with a drainage hole should be selected and filled up to one-fourth with a mixture of fine gravel and *akadama,* in a ratio of one-half to one-half.

5. Unwrap the sheets around the root system carefully, and put the tree in the pot. Afterward, fill the empty space on the sides with the collected original soil mixture mixed with akadama in a ratio of one-half to one-half.

6. Lastly, pour a considerable amount of water over the tree, but take care not to use a fine nozzle so that the soil surface will not be disturbed.

And then? Aftercare.

Place the pot outside, where it is shielded from direct sunlight, and keep it moist but not wet. The tree should be left untouched until the following spring, when it can be trained and repotted for the first time. During the first summer, small amounts of fertilizer can be utilized.

Buying Bonsai Trees

Majority of bonsai lovers started their hobby using a ready-made bonsai tree, purchased in a bonsai store or received as a gift. Although the fun of creating your own tree will not be experienced, it is an incredible way to begin and get a feeling for the fundamental care for bonsai trees. Eventually, you can learn to grow bonsai yourself once you get enthusiastic about them.

Where and How to Buy a Bonsai Tree?

Low-priced bonsai trees are sold in most big garden centers although they are usually of low quality. And at prices that are slightly more expensive, many specialized (online) bonsai stores sell bonsai trees also.

How?

Here is some basic guidance for purchasing bonsai trees:

- It is recommended for beginners to begin with a tree that is easy to care for. Do not begin with purchasing a species of tree that is not easy to care for.

- Only indoor (sub-tropical) trees will do well inside, the same way outdoor trees will only do well when put outside. Purchase a tree that is appropriate for the place where you plan to put it.

- Looking up information about how to properly care for the tree is of high importance, so do not forget to ask what species of tree you purchased.

- Check the pot for any damage.

Choosing Your Tree

These tree species are recommended for you to begin with.

Indoor Bonsai

- Ficus Bonsai
- Jade
- Chinese Elm
- Carmona

Outdoor Bonsai

- Juniper Bonsai
- Ligustrum
- Japanese Maple
- Chinese Elm

The Cheapest and Nicest Ways

Growing a bonsai from seed is a slow and challenging process, but it is also the most rewarding way to go about it. As long as you continue to try and feel passionate about it, the outcome will stun you although it may take a number of years, and you may fail at first.

You'll probably not prefer to wait that long for results if you are a beginner. What most individuals do is purchase a pre-bonsai or look for one in a forest close to your home (do not forget that a pre-bonsai is simply a tree in its early stages). There are numerous considerations in case you decide to go with the second option. You have to get the landowner's permission to do it. Additionally, you have to be extremely careful not to damage the roots when digging. The first weeks of spring are also the specific time to do it.

BONSAI

The planting should be done in autumn, when you grow a bonsai from seed, so germination begins in spring. It's always best to choose trees that can easily adapt to the climate of the place you live in. It'll work in your favor that way.

Chapter 7

Pruning and Trimming

Pruning Bonsai

Pruning a bonsai on a regular basis is certainly the most important approach to train a bonsai. Basically, two different techniques exist. One is maintenance pruning, which is done to maintain and refine a bonsai's existing shape. And the second is structural pruning, which includes more rigorous pruning to give a bonsai tree its fundamental shape or style. Before we progress to discussing both techniques in more detail, looking at some background information on how trees grow is useful. This will enable us to understand how bonsai trees can be pruned in the most efficient way.

Trees undergo "apical dominance," which is a natural tendency to distribute growth to the top (and, to a lesser degree, outer parts of branches). This natural mechanism helps trees to grow higher so as to prevent them from being shaded out by other trees they are in competition with. The tree's inner and lower branches will die eventually when growth is distributed to the top and outer edges while top branches will grow out of proportion—two impacts that are undesirable for bonsai trees' design.

The importance of pruning, as an approach to counter apical dominance, is revealed by the fundamental background. By pruning a tree's top and outer portions more thoroughly, countering apical dominance is achieved, forcing growth to be redistributed to the tree's inner and lower parts.

Bonsai Maintenance Pruning

The objective of doing maintenance pruning is to maintain and refine a tree's shape. Most trees will focus their growth on the top and outer parts of the tree, as explained above. In order to aid growth closer to the internal parts of the tree, it is essential to prune these growth areas on a regular basis.

When to Prune Bonsai?

Maintenance pruning can be carried out all through the growth season, usually from March to September.

How?

As previously mentioned, in order to maintain a tree's shape, maintenance pruning is needed. To achieve this, using twig shears or a normal cutter, just prune branches/shoots that have outgrown the proposed canopy-size/shape. Utilizing the right bonsai tools will be of significant help. It is essential to prune your bonsai—don't be afraid—particularly at the outer and top areas. Prune constantly in order to develop dense foliage and force the tree to distribute growth in a more evenly manner.

Pine trees and a few conifers should be pinched using hands, as opposed to deciduous trees. Pruning some species of conifers with scissors would lead to dead-brown foliage at the cuttings. Hold the tip of the shoot between your thumb and your pointer finger, and pull it away carefully to prevent this from happening. The shoot will snap at its weakest point, and brown ends will not appear. Regarding pruning and pinching, diverse species need different maintenance. Some even require a combination of both.

Defoliation is another method of bonsai pruning. It involves removal of leaves of deciduous trees during summer to make the tree grow new leaves. Ultimately, this technique leads to a decrease in leaf size and an increase in ramification.

Structural Bonsai Pruning

Giving a tree its basic shape regularly involves pruning large branches. It can be difficult to decide on which branches should remain and which branches should be cut off, not just because the action is irreversible but also because it's important in deciding how the tree will end up. You may want to go through the bonsai progressions part of this website, where you will find instances of experienced bonsai growers' structure-pruning nursery stock before learning more about the methods used for pruning bonsai.

When?

Speaking generally, the ideal time to structurally prune a tree is in the early spring, and in some situations, in late autumn (just before and after the growth season). You can check the specifics on a specific tree in the tree species segment, for instance, a Ficus bonsai needs different timing from a Juniper bonsai.

How?

Put the tree on a table at eye level. The first step to take is the removal of all dead wood from the tree. After this, take time to observe your tree closely, and decide which branches do not match the desired design and will need to be cut off.

Ugly scars will be made on the tree as a result of pruning thick branches. However, using a special concave cutter will decrease this effect significantly because of the indentation it creates when removing the branch. A tree that is healthy should have no issues coping with pruning up to one-third of the foliage. Some theories prescribe that after styling a tree, an equal percentage of roots should be cut off or removed. However, most experts agree on performing just one big maintenance each time (or even once per year). This would imply that you structure-prune this spring and hold on with repotting until the following spring (when the tree has recovered completely from the structure pruning).

Lastly, sealing large cuttings using wound paste is advisable. It is available for sale at most (online) bonsai stores. The wounds are protected against infections by the paste, and it aids the tree to heal faster. Again, utilizing the appropriate bonsai tools will be of significant help.

Pruning Bonsai Trees, Step by Step

1. This ficus should be pruned, as numerous long shoots have grown out of shape.
2. Prune long shoots using a twig shear.
3. Cut off about 20 percent of all leaves or the material that was pruned.
4. Use a concave cutter for pruning bigger branches.
5. By pruning the majority of the branch first, make some space to create the cut.
6. Now you have space to create a clean cut exactly where we want it, by cutting off the majority of the branch.

7. The hollow wound is covered with wound paste, which will enhance quick healing of the wound by the tree.

8. You can choose any brand you desire, but we use a wound paste of the Japanese brand.

9. The wound is covered with the wound paste.

Key Takeaway

Postpone structural pruning until the following spring. However, maintenance pruning can be done all throughout the year. One of the approaches to make and shape a bonsai is pruning. It's very vital not to attempt to change too much of the tree's original silhouette. Pruning must be consistent (not only is it necessary to shape but also as a part of the caring process) and to make a beautiful and nice bonsai with strong and plenty of leaves, you ought to have regular spots for them on the tree.

Wiring has also been a valuable option to grow a bonsai on the other hand. All these, shaping angles and making branches, can be done by wiring. It's however very vital to do it the appropriate way because if not done properly, it can turn out to be a disaster.

More techniques that can be used when you grow a bonsai exist. To obtain leaves that are smaller in size or to balance a tree's shape, you can defoliate it. A common technique referred to as *jin and shari* also exists. It consists of making a bonsai look old and mature by making areas of deadwood on the tree, just the way it occurs in nature sometimes.

Growth Principles

1. A plant's growth will move in the general course of the strongest light that is available. By cutting off some of the trunks back to a healthy side branch, trees can be shortened

easily. Eventually, the natural upright position will be assumed by the new leader. By utilizing bonsai wire, alterations can be made to leade direction. Cut back to a bottom twig or bud to reduce a side branch's length. The natural branch design will be maintained as it develops towards the sun (that comes in from the side).

2. If a plant carries more healthy leaves, its growth will be faster and stronger. Lower branches will be the oldest and biggest ideally with other leaves becoming progressively reduced in size and younger nearing the apex. This ideal can come to realization gradually by letting weak lower branches grow overly long and carry additional growth, while the stronger upper branches are cut back tight.

3. Food that is available will be redirected to other growing tips and buds when the extreme twig tip is cut off. The continuous and judicious use of this principle places the power to total control of the tree's growth at your command, even if you cut off four inches or only the tips. The growing tips and food-producing leaves' number and location will dictate the time, place, course, and rate of growth in the whole plant.

4. The survival ability of a growing plant in the absence of photosynthesis is related directly to the measure of food present in the pith rays at the time. Special cells utilized for fluid transportation and food storage are known as pith rays. When leaves are not able to manufacture sufficient sugar required for the tree's immediate needs, excess sugar is stored here for use.

Extra caution should be applied when it comes to pruning a plant whose storage cells are expected to be empty, as a result of leaf drop, resulting from a damage to the root or a recent bout with diseases or insects.

5. Trees that are deciduous depend on food that is stored in the pith rays for the energy required for spring growth. All drastic pruning in the tree's top should be taken care of during the dormant season. Food that has been stored will then go to the desired production of growth. The moment buds start to appear green in the spring is the best time to collect or root-prune. Sugars will move up through the tree and will not be in the pith rays anymore (some of which are situated in the roots).

   Trees that are deciduous will become "twiggier," and if they are forced into a "second spring," they will produce smaller-than-normal leaves. Unless you are sure the tree is in good health, strong, and has been allowed sufficient growth to renew its storage cells, do not try this. In addition, be sure it will have time to fill them up again before another dormant season.

6. The growth of roots will take the course of least resistance in the general direction of the closest source of nutrients and water. Roots hold the trees upright and also anchor it to the ground. Aside from the bark, which experiences disintegration in the moist soil as fast as it forms, they contain similar layers as the trunks and branches. They also react to pruning in a similar manner as limbs and twigs. Small "feeder" roots, which perform the "whole tree" search for nutrients and water, are referred to as root tips.

   Each root tip possesses a protective cap that is pushed forward as the root tip develops and as numerous microscopic root hairs, which probe for and pick up water and nutrients from the soil, are formed. As root tips develop and mature, or when the root cap is harmed or encounters an obstacle which prevents its forward movement, root hairs start to extend themselves to become root tips, with microscopic root hairs and root caps of their own. Soil size and type, in addition to the direction of top growth, provide useful insights to feeder roots' location. Make use of these clues to decide the location of the root ball, which should be dug when collecting.

Make provision for a soil which will encourage the root development that is wanted. Little obstruction is offered by smooth soils; thus, rapid root growth and the development of lesser but larger roots are encouraged. Root ramification and the development of more feeder roots is encouraged by granular soils.

7. Through pruning, root ramification can be induced artificially. To give the tree a look of stability, lift and uncover large surface roots. The bark will also be developed in the process. Then, just underneath the surface of the soil, cut them back sharply to reserve pot space for the more productive feeder roots. This might be achieved over a period of years rather than in one step. Ensure that roots are kept "forever young," and increase their efficiency by intermittent, judicious pruning of roots and repotting in soil that is fresh and viable.

8. At the expense of new foliage, plants will redirect food to flower, fruit, or production of seed. Do not let this happen if the plant is not strong.

9. A tree will kill off a piece of itself if under extreme stress. By keeping the tree healthy, it guarantees that you will be the one to make the decision of parts that should live and parts that will need to be sacrificed.

10. A distinct interrelationship exists between top growth and root growth, not just to size but also as to direction. Root pruning lessens the demand for food from the leaves while top pruning lessens the demands for raw products from the roots. As long as a balance is maintained, the tree will remain small and in good health.

11. The growth habit and general adult shape of a tree depend on its species (hereditary blueprint). Never try to style a tree in a way which is entirely alien to its nature. The tree will fight you till the end of time. The individuals who are great at styling have carried out studies on trees as they exist and grow in nature, as well as how they react to different environmental pressures.

Chapter 8

Wiring

Attitude

Obtain some wire and test. Try branches from your yard if you are being careful about wiring your bonsai. Don't wait till you are certain you can do it right. This is an example of those "creep before you walk and walk before you run" sort of activities. You will not become comfortable with wiring by watching another person do it, sort of like figuring how to drive a car. Keep in mind that far fewer bonsai will exist on the earth, even in the Orient, if less-than-perfect wiring killed most trees. Give yourself time to enjoy the process and consider alternatives, except when you make it a race. Bonsai wiring is not a race.

Why Spiral Wire?

Bonsai can be made without wiring, yes. Repositioning tons of trunks and branches can be carried out by using "spreaders" and

BONSAI

guying with rope or wire. A spiraled wire can, however, be an incredibly valuable tool, giving the bonsai producer far greater control and offering more choices in changing directions of branches and making pleasing curves.

Aesthetic gain is regularly as simple as wiring down outward jutting branches, and bringing the foliage at the ends of these branches nearer to the tree's trunk in the process. The tree's trunk appears bigger and more impressive, with this narrowing of the tree's silhouette.

As an alternative option or as an enhancement to swinging branches down, trunks and branches can be significantly shortened, once again bringing foliage nearer to the soil or trunk, by utilizing wires to introduce curves.

Do this personally by cutting a straight wire of six or eight inches in length then by snaking it back and forth a bit, give it one or two curves. You will now observe that the distance between the cut ends is considerably shorter. Yes, extreme bending toward the spiraling of a pig's tail can have the effect of extreme compression of the height, branch length, and foliage mass of the tree.

The spiraled wire can create possible repositioning on upper branches on wood that is not excessively mature and stiff. This can be possible by twisting the upper part of a young tree's trunk to the point where it can swing a branch 180 degrees from left to right or vice versa, practically placing it on the other side of the tree. By swinging down its initial leader and putting up a lower and shorter side branch, making it the new leader, spiraled wire can shorten (and widen) your tree top.

Furthermore, strong growth of a tree's overactive parts can be controlled using wiring. The growth of the wired part will be lessened by wiring alone. Lowering the limbs toward the horizontal, and even farther away from vertical, will, however, have an increasingly greater effect the farther the branch is moved in slowing down the lowered part's growth. In this manner, wiring can be a valuable supplement to pruning in growth limitation. Suggestions have even been made that wiring can aid in flowering promotion on reluctant trees.

Thinking Ahead

Some differences exist between conifers and deciduous trees. The broad pattern is that conifers are tolerant of bending and have a tendency to be more flexible, even if the wood is fairly mature, than deciduous trees, which become more brittle and cannot tolerate bending as they age. Also, the majority of deciduous trees that are healthy can be cut back to interesting stumps, with no remainder of foliage, and they will recover. This is unlike conifers, whose branches normally die if all their foliage is cut off. Also, remember that wiring is a stress that the tree must utilize energy stored as reserves in recovering from it. On a tree that isn't strong, do only a little or no wiring at all.

First, make it healthy. After this, think about how much other stress, for instance, heavy pruning, potting, or repotting, you have plans for at the same time. The Japanese state that heavy wiring and repotting at the same time are extremely dangerous. Wait for one year between major stresses. Allowing brittle-wooded trees, such as azaleas, for instance, dry out one day or two before wiring is regularly recommended. The branches are more flexible this way. But caution is encouraged to avoid drying to the point of harm. Placing the plant out of the wind and direct sunlight after it starts to get dry will be of help.

Before starting any extensive wiring, a careful cleaning will make the work less difficult. Dispose of all dead foliage, weak growth not essential to the tree's structure (the weakest branches do not become strong), and on pine trees, remove all needles that are over a year old. This is also an ideal time to dispose of any misdirected growth below a branch or shooting straight up perhaps, that can't be redirected in a valuable way. Exercising through continued flexing of hard to bend wood and soften it up before applying wire is frequently suggested by individuals with a great deal of experience. This means about five to ten minutes or even more is devoted to massaging heavy wood. In the extreme, this can also imply twisting the branch to be bent.

Timing

Wiring can be carried out almost all year round on majority of species in more temperate climates, such as in much of Japan and California. Pine wiring is restricted to the dormant season in Japan, from the first fall color to the first cherry blooms. Repotting season ("when the sap is ascending," after the ground has thawed and before new shoots are developing) is also prime time for wiring in our climate. The worst candidate for wiring is the tree that supports a lot of soft growth, as with repotting.

Late-season wiring, without permitting recovery time before freezing starts, is best stayed away from because winter cold and frozen soil bring immense stress to all plants. Any tree wintered where its soil will not freeze will be an exception. Therefore, our late-season window of wiring opportunity is around August to September. A great time for wiring to set new shoots at a satisfying angle and to slow down shoot growth for numerous, fast-growing, brittle-wooded species, like maple, azalea, wisteria, ginkgo, and crabapple, is late June to early July, when leaves are nearly in full size and the new shoots are starting to stiffen but not yet extremely weak. When pruning of leaf (defoliation) is carried out in June on maples, wiring, soon after defoliation, can function well.

Aluminum versus Copper Wire

Both aluminum and copper wire have been well used in wiring bonsai, and both have their detractors and supporters. Well-annealed copper wire is sufficiently soft to apply easily than when flexed. It "work hardens" (the aftereffect of its crystal structure's disruption), giving it holding power, well past its original strength. In carrying out the heavy-bending that is possible on conifers, this stiffening comes in handy. To produce a similar holding power, a larger diameter of aluminum wire is needed due to the fact that aluminum wire is softer and does not work harden like copper. It's been most prominent in carrying out lighter wiring, particularly on delicate-barked trees, such as maples and azaleas. Wrapping wire using spiraling strips of light paper around it to protect the bark of sensitive plants is regularly recommended by the Japanese.

Wire Thickness

Although numerous guidelines have been proposed, the best approach appears to be making an attempt to flex the trunk or branch to bend it then flex the available wire, and select a wire that offers more resistance than the tree. In doing this, remember that utilizing wire a little heavier than you really require will work better at all times than using wire not strong enough to hold things where you want them. Obviously, adding an extra wire or two, parallel and near the first, will often work if the wire you made use of wasn't strong enough. When you need to hold the wired branch in position, don't make hesitations to add a guy wire attached by anchoring it to the branch wire.

Wiring Sequence

Following the way a tree grows is the standard procedure. Beginning at soil level, wire the trunk first then work upward toward its tip. Then wire the branches, beginning with the lowest and heaviest. Afterward, do secondary and tertiary branches. Complete it with fine wiring of branch tips and the apex of the tree. Note that all this translates to is that the thickest wire is applied first, followed by the next thickest, etc. while the thinnest wire is put on last, during refining.

How Long Do You Cut the Wire?

It appears difficult for some of us to accept the inarguable truth that one can cut a really long wire short, but a really short wire can't be cut long. Cutting the wire not less than a third longer than the distance to be wired will save wire and time.

Adequate Anchoring

In wiring, this is one of the greatest challenges. The issue, essentially, is securing one end of a wire so that it doesn't slip or move as the wrapping proceeds before coiling whatever is left of it into position. This can be as straightforward as using the end of the wire to wrap around a branch stub or the base of a separate branch. The wire's end is normally thrust straight down into the soil, at the tree's base, in wiring a tree's trunk, so unwanted movement will be prevented by its roots. However, the most effective method of anchoring branch wires by far is to utilize one wire to wrap two branches, one end being spiraled out of one branch, and the opposite end, after a total wrap (or two if possible) around the trunk, being spiraled out another branch, requiring a similar-sized wire.

When there is no apparent way to handle a branch, either making use of a wire secured in the soil and making a few passes around the tree's trunk or making use of a wire's end from another branch, a valuable technique is to make use of doubled wire to do the separated branch. Cut wire double the length you would use ordinarily. Bend it two times. Begin with the bend behind the trunk (far from the branch), then wrap the two ends outward and parallel on the branch, using one end to make a secondary branch if possible. In numerous cases, especially when proceeding with thinner wire after utilizing heavier wire to part way out of a branch, the lighter wire's end can be secured by passing it through any large-enough gap between the branch and the heavy wire.

The Spiraling Process

Practice how to hold the last wrap of wire with the thumb and index finger of the left hand while "pushing" the next wire coil into place using the fingertips of the right hand. Also, the left hand's "free fingers" are utilized for twigs and foliage separation, as is required to make a way for the wrap being applied. (Of course, in doing left-handed wiring, the hands are reversed.) Advance the left hand each time the wire goes underneath the branch. Have imaginations of coiling a garden hose. Wrapping the branch with absolutely no pressure placed on its bark is your goal.

So by giving it a slight twist and "push" (back toward the base of the branch that is being wired) as you work, before the wire makes contact with the branch, you are attempting to put a bend into it. Picture a slight back pressure that attempts to compress instead of stretching the wire being applied while the wire is being rotated at the same time. If wiring clockwise, twist the wire clockwise. If wiring counterclockwise, twist the wire counterclockwise.

In case you find this rotation or twisting of the wire hard to imagine, try to imagine the unused wire is a snake with a narrow, long stripe running down the length of its back. Then understand that, so that its stripe turns a spiraling line, what you do with the wire as you wrap it is just like twisting that snake. If you work with the branch that is being wired, pointed nearly directly toward you, you will find this spiraling process a lot less demanding.

How tight is this wire wrapped? Once again, laying the wire around the branch, with no pressure, is the goal. The Japanese state that enough space should be left to allow a strip of rice paper slip between the wire and the branch. Apparently, when a branch is bent, there will be contact on the pressure points. Leave additional room between the wire and the branch.

Adding the smaller wires will be less difficult, especially when you are consistent in laying the passing wrap on the trunk's surface, directly opposite where the branch is attached, parallel to the big wire, and running them out the laterals without a lot of crossing wires. Utilize a branched stick from your landscape to experiment a bit with this method, and you will find out that it gives the wirer incredible freedom.

Care after Wiring

Keep it in mind that wiring is stressful, and thorough wiring is very stressful to a tree. Ensure that the heavily wired tree is protected in the same manner you would protect a freshly potted tree. Keep it away from wind and direct sunlight for five to ten days, depending on the severity of wiring, and wet the leaves as often as two or three times each day if possible. This is not the period to add further stress by pruning, fertilization, or applying the pesticide. Be very careful with watering as well. Do not let the soil become dry, but don't keep it full of water constantly either.

When Do You Take the Wire Off?

You do this just before the wire cuts into the tree. Growth sets branches in their new positions, and growth (thickening) results in wire cutting into the tree. Watch out, in particular, for wire cutting in on the shoots that are most vigorous (the shoots highest in the tree) and at bases of the branch where the wire will be tight and the branch thickens fast. Let the wire stay for longer if you find no evidence of cutting in. If you remove the wire and the tree appears weak, allow it some recovery time. After this, rewire anything that has not stayed where you need it. Even when it comes to maintaining really old bonsai, the process is continuous.

Finally

As a matter of fact, I have the impression that most of the very proficient bonsai wirers follow these rules without needing to put them into words. Instead, they rely on sound instincts they have acquired through lots of practice. The objective here is to help individuals who don't have these instincts to practice on their own, using these ideas.

Chapter 9

Watering and Fertilizing

Watering

They say bonsai die faster due to improper watering than any other cause, with "overwatering" responsible for a huge number of these deaths. This is true. The moment the surface of the soil feels dry to the touch, add water. Do not stop until the entire root ball is wet, and *don't* water again till the surface of the soil feels dry again. This could be done either three times a day or every three days, depending on several factors, like the time of the year, the health of the plant, and the composition of the soil.

This raises the question, "Is the soil bone-dry, wet, soggy, or moist?"

Bone-Dry: Moisture is completely absent from the soil. Even though some plants, like Japanese black pine, boxwood, junipers, and sand pine like their soil a bit dry, no plant can survive a bone-dry condition for a long time.

Wet: This is the point of saturation in granular soil, particles stick but separate too easily. Wet soils are ideal for bog plants, like tupelo, cypress, and maple. If the soil stays saturated for a long period, the problem should be identified. It could either be due to poor pot drainage or because the plant's roots are not functioning properly. Find the issue, and fix it immediately.

Soggy: This is the point of saturation for, clay, muck, and other soils with small grain. When it is squeezed together, the soil packs into a solid ball. A soggy soil gives room for no airspace, and the plants drown, literally.

Moist: The soil feels cool when touched and is crumbly and loose. Moist conditions are the safest and the best condition for most plants.

It is important to note that after the plant's foliage has been misted, the soil gives a deceivingly moist feeling, but underneath, it may be dangerously dry. Be aware of this.

Caution: While allowing your bonsai to become bone-dry, never sink it into a pan of water in an attempt to get the entire root ball wet. It's more advisable to mist the foliage lightly then place the plant in the shade until evening. At this point, take the plant back to its regular spot, and leave the morning dew to revive the fibrous roots while you continue watering as you've been doing.

Here are the five key points to remember when watering your bonsai:

1. Newly potted plants demand less water than established ones.

2. Plants in small pots are to be watered more frequently.

3. The bigger the size of the leaves, the more water the plant

needs.

4. The need for water will be necessitated by a hot sun or windy weather.

5. During winter or dormancy, less water is required.

Fertilizer

Fertilizer is not plant food. It is any substance that contains plant nutrients and is added to the plant's environment. Normally, these fertilizers are added to the soil or water; however, some fertilizers can be sprayed onto the plant leaves directly or into the air.

Even though it's common for many fertilizers to be referred to as plant food, this has never been its proper description. Plants manufacture their own food with water, carbon dioxide, and solar energy. This food consists of sugars and carbohydrates, which is then combined with the plant nutrients in producing vitamins, enzymes, and proteins, along with other things vital for plant growth.

NPK

N: Nitrogen is essential for the green color and new growth in plants. Plants need nitrogen for cell division and manufacturing of protein.

P: Phosphorus plays a role in flowering and good root growth.

K: Potassium is responsible for healthy cell activity.

A Balanced Fertilizer

When the numbers of NPK are equal, it is referred to as a balanced fertilizer. This is needed for total overall growth and health for most cultivation purposes, including bonsai.

You might be wondering if a 20-20-20 fertilizer is better than 10-10-10. And what do these numbers stand for? No, the directions for use considers the different percentages of dry weight. This is to say you will use half as much as 20-20-20 per gallon of the solution as 10-10-10.

These figures represent the percentage of available nitrogen, phosphorus, and potassium (N-P-K) present in the bag. So, in 12-8-10 fertilizers, you will find 12 percent nitrogen, 8 percent phosphorus, and 10 percent potassium.

For many bonsai, we advise you to regularly apply a low percentage of fertilizer like 5-5-5 or something close to this. Apply it this way the entire year. An increase in the percentage of fertilizer applied could lead to growth spurts and could burn the roots of our potted trees.

Having said that, during the period of late winter to early spring, most bonsai farmers use a 10-10-10 on some trees to accelerate growth. Do this only when you know how the plants would react. Again, consider slow-release against fast-release fertilizers. Bonsai farmers pick slow-release organics instead of the fast-release chemical varieties.

Macronutrients and Micronutrient

The elements an organism needs in large quantities to live and grow are referred to as macronutrients. Nitrogen (N), phosphorous, (P) and potassium (K) are examples of macronutrients. On the other hand, elements required by plants in small quantities for their survival and growth are called micronutrients. They include cobalt, copper, iron, boron, manganese, molybdenum and zinc.

In the absence of macronutrients, there is a reduction in the growth rate of plants, just like a deficiency in vitamins in some humans. Most fertilizers publicize that they contain micronutrients. Please pick one of these instead of the "regular" version.

When Should You Fertilize?

The trick about knowing when to fertilize your plants is to understand their growing cycle. This cycle has three stages—growth stage, fruiting stage, and dormant stage.

Growth Stage. Plants require more nitrogen and phosphorous while growing. Nitrogen aids leafy growth and encourages the growth of plant stem and branches. They need phosphorus for seed germination and root development.

Fruiting Stage. When a plant steps into the fruiting stage, the demand for a generous amount of potassium shoots up. Plants need potassium because it enables them to produce fruits and flowers while also aiding them in their resistance to pests and diseases.

Dormant Stage. When plants enter hibernation, their need for fertilization drops. Some amount of phosphorus will help strengthen the root before the plant enters dormancy. This is why we use a 0-10-10 during dormant seasons to enhance root growth.

What Kind Fertilizer Should You Use?

There exist so many opinions about fertilizers in the world of bonsai farming. The simplest solution for many farmers is the use of a timed-release fertilizer, like Osmocote. The benefit of this is that, any time you water, bits of fertilizer dissolve and feed your tree. However, these fertilizers typically don't release nutrients when the weather is cooler than ninety degrees and release lots of nutrients when the weather is warmer than seventy degrees. No good will come to you when it's cool, so you'll need another kind of fertilizer. During heat, there is the risk of a fertilizer burn, so remove some of those pellets in late summer.

It's highly recommended to start fertilization in late February or early March. In pines, after the candles are removed, more fertilizer should be applied.

Pot Size	How Much Osmocote to Use
Large (> 12" diameter)	4–8 tablespoons
Medium (e.g., 12" diameter)	2–4 tablespoons
Small (e.g., 4" diameter)	2–3 teaspoons

An Osmocote package says it's good for six months. The truth, however, is that it does not last more than a few months when applied to bonsai because you would water it so frequently. Therefore, there is the need to refill it every couple of months. To get a fast fertilizer boost, some farmers make use of the diluted version of Miracle-Gro or Miracid on pines and azaleas. Fish emulsion is also preferred by some people because it's considered "safer" even though it attracts wildlife and smells nasty.

There is so much nitrogen in Osmocote than what is required to be used during the dormant stage. We recommend the following as alternatives.

    a. For fruit-bearing and flowering trees which produce berries, apply low nitrogen fertilizer (find bulb and bloom fertilizer) or seaweed extract when watering.

b. For deciduous trees. Use 0-10-10, like E. B. Stone Ultra Bloom.

How Much Fertilizer to Use

Plants you want to grow larger and younger plants require more fertilizer (mostly nitrogen) than the older trees you've been maintaining. An accurate guide is to use a tablespoon or two of Osmocote on trees growing in medium-sized pots (e.g., twelve to eighteen inches long). Use a teaspoon when applying to smaller trees.

In rainy seasons, fertilizer washes out more quickly. It's, therefore, a brilliant idea to use extra fertilizer, perhaps two times the recommended quantity of Osmocote. This is safe since low nitrogen fertilizer doesn't "burn," like too much Osmocote.

When to Change the Fertilizer?

Watering Osmocote every day ensures that the pellets won't last more than a few months. There is, therefore, a need to observe these pellets regularly to check if they are still full. The pellets seen are, in reality, a plastic bead that contains the fertilizer. When the fertilizer leaches away, it leaves an empty plastic bead. You know the time for removals and replacements has come if you can crush these beads with your fingers.

As stated earlier on, in hot temperatures, remove some of these pellets. When the weather cools and trees enter their dormant stages, replace the high-nitrogen fertilizer with blooming fertilizer.

Chlorosis: Yellowing of Leaves

The location of the yellowing will identify the problem.

- On younger leaves: Shows lack of iron or manganese.
- On older leaves: Shows lack of nitrogen or potassium.
- On all the leaves: Shows a lack of nutrients. Fertilize it.
- Between the veins: Shows lack of iron and magnesium.
- At the edge of the leaf: Shows an absence of magnesium and potassium.

Nitrogen deficiency shows up as chlorosis of the entire plant, turning the leaves and needles yellow. It shows up most times on the leaves and needles first. Fixing it quickly would require a liquid fertilizer.

Phosphorus deficiency causes a variety of symptoms that are not easy to point out. A change in color of the stem or underside, or a gray or brown-netted veining shows a deficiency in phosphorous.

Magnesium deficiency shows up as chlorosis of the tip of the needles. When the yellowing is noticed mostly on new growth, then it's caused by an iron deficiency. If magnesium is lacking, sprinkle a teaspoon of Epsom salt to the top of the soil. Since Epsom salt dissolves very fast, you'll have to repeat this sprinkling a few times over a month. If iron is the deficient nutrient, sprinkle a tablespoon of Ironite at the top of the soil. It dissolves slowly, and applying once is usually enough.

Too Much Fertilizer

The same way a lack of fertilizer or a little of it could cause a problem, excess fertilizer can lead to a "burn." A dry-brown edge on the leaves is the classic symptom. A brown coloring in leaves could also be a result of too much heat and poor watering, so be careful when determining the issue here. After ruling out heat as the current cause of the problem, evaluate the amount of fertilizer at the top of the soil. If the fertilizer looks like it's more than the recommended amount given up there, remove most of it for a week or two and give time for the excess to leach away from the soil and for the tree to start healing.

You might want to add some new fertilizer, but keep the total amount less than the previous quantity that led to a burning. First and foremost, check if the fertilizer beads actually have fertilizer in them. Should they be empty, then it's time to remove the used-up fertilizer and apply a new one immediately.

The moment a leaf burns, it never recovers. So shield the plants from heat while you fertilize, and water in the proper quantities to prevent the leaves from burning in the first instance.

Chapter 10

Seasonal Care

What Makes a Good Bonsai

- A few signs of stability and good health, like leaf color and well-settled, natural-looking moss. The absence of signs of carelessness and abuse, like scars from a wire left on too long or badly healed pruning scars.

- A strong, properly shaped trunk growing naturally from the soil and moving upward toward the top in an even taper.

- A proper fanning out of surface roots (*nebari*) from the trunk's base until it disappears gradually into the soil.

- A well-proportioned head of branches, well-spaced, and appears to naturally spring from the trunk or bigger branches.

- The tree looks as natural as possible when you consider its style, size, and species.

- The pot is proportional to the tree in forming artistic synchrony.

- The tree must be in the pot to create a visual balance

- Flowers, leaves, and fruits must remain in proportion.

- The tree, springing with some of its roots clinging to a rock, must really hold fast to the rock and not just wrap it around.

- A tree should be planted, properly raised from its pot so that the bole can be seen clearly over the rim of the pot when viewed at eye level.

- Moss, stones, or any other covering on the soil surface looks natural and in scale.

Before Bonsai Training

The severe top and root pruning needed to change an ordinary plant into a bonsai is a shock to the plant and may lead to its death. The guidelines below will increase its survival chances.

1. **Take off the excess soil above the roots on the surface.** Excess soil at the base of the trunk is not good for the plant.

2. **Check plants for signs of disease or insect, and treat promptly.** Don't attempt training your tree till you are certain that it has recovered its health and vigor.

3. **Ensure your plant never gets bone-dry.** Little feeder roots that are necessary for the plants' survival could be damaged beyond repair if the plant gets bone-dry.

4. **Fertilize regularly during the growing season.** The quantity and type of fertilizer depend on personal choices

and situations.

5. **Apply a special booster fertilizer about three weeks before training.** The ability to survive would depend on the plant's inner strength, with dormant deciduous trees being an exception.

6. **In the twenty-four hours that precede a pruning and wiring session, leave the soil to become dry.** This makes the trunk and branches more pliable and less likely to be broken during wiring.

7. **Same as above, before root pruning and potting.** Dry soil gets easily broken up, with less resultant damage to the fresh roots.

8. **Make a place for your new bonsai.** The best site depends on the particular plant species to be used and the local circumstances.

9. Do your own research on the tree's needs.

After Drastic Pruning and Potting

1. The soil to be used should be slightly and evenly moist (cool to the touch). Fibrous roots become dehydrated while cleaning and pruning. Avoid saturating the soil immediately after potting. It's rather advisable to mist the foliage and place it in a shade.

2. Water it thoroughly the following morning with a Superthrive solution (ten drops to a gallon of water). Place the tree in some temporary location to receive an adequate air circulation and good light. Endeavor to protect it from direct sunlight, freezing weather, and strong winds. Do not

move the plant until it's absolutely necessary.

3. Mist the foliage several times daily. Water as needed while watching out carefully for the following:

    a. Signs of stress. Observe for leaf drop or wilting on broadleaf plants, including being dry-looking and having limp foliage on evergreens, and browning buds or twig tips. Water every week with Superthrive.

    b. Signs of new vigor. Look for fresh buds on broadleaf plants showing green, and fresh, light-green growth on evergreen. The soil suddenly dries out quicker than normal. This is a sign that new roots are functioning. Begin hardening off.

4. Hardening off (returning gradually to normal). Start exposing the tree to direct sunlight early in the mornings, and increase these periods of direct exposure gradually till the plant receives its full quota. If you notice any signs of stress, reduce exposure time a bit, but don't return to complete shade. Wait a week then try again.

5. If nursing your bonsai tree becomes a success through the first three months, *Congratulations*. There are chances it will live to a ripe, old age.

6. If you weren't successful, trace the roots of your lack of success. Examine the circumstances. Ask for help in analyzing the reasons for the death of your tree. Take notes from the experience then try again, with better luck this time!

Winter-Time Care for Bonsai Trees

BONSAI

Introduced to the United States by Japanese immigrants in the early 1900s, the art of bonsai makes small-scale replicas of full-grown and aged trees. Bonsai are trees that should be grown outdoors in all seasons. They are not house plants. In the absence of the winter temperatures, bonsai trees will live only a few years. Tropical and subtropical bonsai trees are special cases that need extra protection.

Normal Wintering

Tree species that are hardy (able to survive during winter) down to US Department of Agriculture hardiness zone 6 and below, like spruce (*Picea sp.*) and Japanese maple (*Acer palmatum*), are meant to be left outdoors during the winter. These trees need a period of dormancy to stay healthy. At the end of the growing season, the tree gets set for the winter by hardening stems and storing sugars, which act as antifreeze. When the temperature drops below fifty degrees Fahrenheit, the tree enters the dormant stage and is never damaged or affected by the cold.

When the water in the pot freezes, the roots don't. Uncontrolled winds, which dehydrate the tree, and overwatering from the rain or melting snow could be an issue. Think of placing trees in sheltered places, away from snowfall and wind. After their leaves have dropped, deciduous trees don't need any more light. Evergreen trees need more light but not sustained, direct light, which causes damage.

Below Fifteen Degrees

The story changes completely if the temperature reaches fifteen degrees Fahrenheit. A weather as extreme as this will damage the tree if it is not protected. Bring the trees into shelters or garages, where temperatures stay above fifteen degrees but below fifty degrees Fahrenheit. When the trees get warmed, above fifty degrees, they come out of dormancy and won't remain healthy.

Bonsai trees that are hardy only to USDA zone 7, like the trident maple (*Acer buergerianum*) and Chinese elm (*Ulmus parvifolia*), will find the shelter beneficial, even at twenty-three degrees Fahrenheit. Clear all moss, algae, and surface debris from the bonsai pot when placing the tree inside a shelter. They have the ability to harbor pests and fungi, which causes extensive damages in sheltered environments. A bonsai farmer in Alaska reports protecting his bonsai from extreme temperatures by covering them in deep snow. The snow ensures the plants stay at a freezing temperature while also insulating them from colder temperatures.

Watering and Fertilizer

Don't ever allow the bonsai growing medium to dry out. Winter-water consumption is very low; however, bonsai tree roots still require a damp soil (not drenched). Trees that remain outside could be over-washed by melting snow and rain while winds can cause the moisture to evaporate quickly at low temperatures. So endeavor to check your trees and don't expose them unnecessarily to the elements. Bonsai trees brought inside or placed in coverings need to be watered as little as two to three times every winter, so this is one task that is easy to forget. Don't apply any fertilizer from late autumn to early spring.

Tropical and Subtropical Bonsai

These bonsai trees are hardy only to USDA zone 8 and above. These bonsai trees are meant to be kept above fifty degrees Fahrenheit the entire year, with little sunlight. Bring them inside during winter and give them dedicated growing lamps to keep them healthy if they can't stay in a window with enough sunlight. Water them continuously, like twice a day or more. A steady watering eases the burden of subtropical and wintering tropical bonsai trees.

Summer Bonsai Tree Care

Growing a bonsai tree is a year-round commitment. Although you might have less maintenance to do in summer, there's still a need to keep an eye on your bonsai during this volatile season. Every species of bonsai needs special care during the summer, which differs from the rest. For most parts, however, there's a need to watch their temperature, humidity, and growth.

Temperature

Move your bonsai outdoors in the summer, but never leave them out of the house for three months, and expect to meet a living bonsai when you return. Should you be staying in an area which heats up during the day and cools at night, bring that bonsai indoors at night.

If the heat rises to alarming levels, and your bonsai tree is not a tropical species, still bring it in at night. Due to an increase in light and heat, there's a need to water your bonsai tree more often. If there is a need to spray your bonsai tree with a nontoxic, environmentally friendly pesticide, never do so when the sun is high.

Humidity

The right humidity levels are a concern for summer care of your bonsai tree. You won't have to bother so much about humidity levels when your bonsai tree is outside, and it's humid. What bothers you is dry air in the house, which happens with air-conditioning. Keep your bonsai tree away from a draft, as this could dry it out.

Misting your bonsai tree is a great way to counter dry air as opposed to a full watering. Pour water to fill a plastic misting spray bottle, and give the bonsai a going over as often as desired. The use of humidity trays or pebble trays is another good way of keeping dry air from harming your bonsai. These are just shallow trays, with pebbles and water at the base. The water in the pebble tray should not touch the bottom of your bonsai's pot.

Growth

The season for rampant growth among plants is summer though it may not be helpful or beneficial to a bonsai tree. Prune the roots in spring. There's also need to constantly check for sudden growth that may quickly turn your bonsai into a full-sized tree. Weekly pinching and pruning of your bonsai tree depend on the species of bonsai you are growing.

Caring for an Evergreen Bonsai Tree

The evergreen is considered the least tasking to grow.

Follow these easy guidelines listed below to ensure your evergreen bonsai transforms into a masterpiece you will always remain proud of.

Watering

When watering an evergreen, never forget that most varieties tend to tolerate dryness better than over-watering.

Bearing that in mind, supply your bonsai with water every three days or so. It's definitely a better option to slightly underwater an evergreen than to over-water it.

Whenever the needles of your evergreen specimen turn brown, increase the humidity by applying a gentle mist of water.

Fertilizing

It is really important to fertilize your growing evergreens to make it healthy in order to go through all the stress of training and pruning successfully.

The common principle for proper fertilization of evergreens includes applying a high-nitrogen fertilizer twice a month, in the spring and early summer.

It is enough to fertilize twice a month from mid- to late summer. At the beginning of fall and throughout the winter period, fertilize seldom (like once in a month or so).

Pruning

Evergreen species are not really demanding in terms of pruning, and they generally need the application of pruning techniques mainly during autumn. In spring and summer, evergreen bonsai stays focused on supporting new growth.

Endeavor to use carefully sterilized shears in pruning your bonsai. This is because evergreens are extremely susceptible to diseases, some of which could be found on the surface of your pruning tools.

Sunlight

It's common knowledge that most evergreens are lovers of plenty and direct sunlight. Keeping an evergreen bonsai tree on a generously sunlit window is a perfect idea.

For outdoor growing, it's necessary to protect your evergreen bonsai from severe winds, as they could get knocked down and die at the end of a sudden storm.

Another reward you can expect from an evergreen specimen: cones!

Although tiny in size, bonsai evergreen produces cones like every other evergreen tree. These cones are smaller in size than those of the regular evergreen trees and will drop off at some point during the year, containing little seeds.

That said, increasing the size of your evergreen bonsai garden is a simple yet inexpensive task.

Some specimens of evergreens which produce cones are, juniper, needle, silver fir, and a variety of spruce trees, among others.

Rules of Bonsai

Trunk and Nebari Rules

1. Height must be six times the caliper of the trunk.
2. Leave the trunk to lean slightly toward the viewer.
3. Let the trunk flare at the base to visually anchor the plant.
4. The roots should radiate from the flare.
5. Don't leave eye-poking roots (directly at the viewer).
6. Leave the apex to lean toward the viewer.
7. The trunk is meant to taper as it rises, not a reverse taper.
8. During grafting, match the stock and scion properly so that

they are unobtrusive or could be placed low enough to disappear into the *nebari*. Curves at the trunk should never result in "pigeon breast" (roundness toward the viewer).

9. The apex should finish in the direction set by the base. Maintain the flow.

10. The trunk line shouldn't be allowed to move back on itself. This relates to the flow of the tree. Any trunk line which moves back on itself creates a C-curve.

11. The apex should stay above the base, for formal and informal upright.

12. Too many S-curves will be tiresome in informal uprights.

13. While growing the tree, the curves should stay closer together (related to branch placement).

14. One apex to one tree.

15. Twin tree trunks should be divided at the base, not higher up.

Branches

1. No crossing of branches or branches that cross the trunk.

2. No eye-poking branches (branches pointed directly at the receiver).

3. The first branch should be positioned almost one-third of the tree.

4. The branches that follow must be placed at one-third of the remaining distance to the top of the tree.

BONSAI

5. No belly branches. (Branches should go on the outside of the curves.)

6. Branch caliper should be a fraction of the trunk. Branches thicker than one-third will result in the trunk caliper being too thick.

7. The first branch stays at the left (or right), the next branch right (left), and the third branch should be at the back.

8. Let the branches alternate visually. There should be no parallel branches.

9. There should be a decrease in size and calipers of branches as they ascend.

10. Leave spaces between the branches to "allow birds to fly through."

11. Place the first and second branches (left and right) forward of the midline to "attract" the viewer.

12. The first, second, and third branches should be roughly 120 degrees apart, with the back branch not directly behind the tree.

13. One branch to one trunk position, no "wheel and spoke" or whorled branches, or bar branches (directly opposite to each other).

14. The branches should form the outlines of a scalene triangle, with the apex representing God. The middle corner represents man while the lower corner stands for earth.

15. Secondary branches should interchange left and right. Follow the rules of main branch placement, except no secondary branch should be moving up or down. This

creates the foliage pad.

16. In order to create the illusion of an old tree, wire down the branches. Growing trees have ascending branches. The branches near and at the top could be horizontal or ascending since it is the young part of the tree.

17. In general, branches for cascades follow the rule for uprights except that the trunk moves down.

18. For twin trees, there shouldn't be branches which would cross the trunk between the trees. The triangle of foliage is created by the outside branches of both trees.

19. The foliage should not hide the *jin*.

Pots

1. Place the tree behind the midline of the pot and to the right or left of the center line.

2. The caliper of the trunk should be the depth of the trunk, except for cascades.

3. Use colored glazed pots for flowering and fruit-bearing trees. Let the color of the pot complement the flower color.

4. Make the width of the pot two-thirds the height of the tree. And the width, in very short trees, should be two-thirds the spread of the tree.

5. Match the style of the pot to the tree. Uprights with limited movements should be placed in rectangular pots. Informal uprights with plenty trunk movement should stay in oval or round pots. Large trees should be kept in deep, rectangular pots.

BONSAI

Culture

1. Keep soils in uniform not layered.

2. Full-strength fertilization needed.

3. Watering should be from above and not by submerging. This prevents the buildup of salts.

4. Don't mist. Raise the humidity by using a tray of pebbles and water or by keeping the area under the bench wet.

5. Extract most of the "fines" from the soil mix. Use coarse particles only.

6. Watering should be done only when the plants need to be watered. Do not follow a fixed schedule.

7. Temperate climate plants should remain outside. Tropical and subtropical plants alone are suitable for indoor bonsai. Give temperate climate plants an appropriate period of cold dormancy if they are to stay indoors.

Chapter 11

Repotting

Growing a bonsai (Japanese for potted plant, or *penjing*, Chinese for potted scene), means taking the organism from the nurturing earth and placing it in a confined space. The plant no longer receives nutrients from the earth and life-giving rain too. You assume the role of a caregiver, a guardian, and an all-powerful God to these potted bonsai trees. So then it is necessary to understand and to assume the responsibility, the obligation to all your potted bonsai plants, as they are now at your mercy. Therefore, attend properly to the needs of your living art creatures by becoming a merciful, omniscient being.

Why Repot Your Bonsai?

Apart from watering, pruning, feeding, and training, repotting is one of the biggest tasks any bonsai tender needs to get acquainted with while performing on a regular basis. The question then is, what purpose does repotting serve? Why do we do it?

The answer relates directly to your first responsibility since you have taken the tree/plant away from the nurturing earth. In natural environments, plants have ample amount of spaces to spread their roots and absorb untold nutrients from the earth. In confined pots, however, depending on the kind of soil mix you have, the soil decomposes slowly, and the roots fill the pots. If you don't prune the roots and introduce fresh material, then get ready for a disaster.

Root Bound

Around the tenth- to eleventh-century Song dynastic period in ancient China, foot-binding was common among the upper crust of the society. The reasoning behind this tradition is mainly due to not allowing the woman to do any strenuous labor. However, the aesthetic purpose behind foot-binding was because it makes the foot look delicately small and pretty, and this was in high demand.

The Chinese phrase "要靚不要命" loosely translated to as "Desire beauty instead of a good, healthy life." Here is how this correlates to bonsai. Just like foot-binding, binding the roots is just as dangerous to the tree as it is to a woman. Growth is inhibited, and movement is hindered. This could cause negative effects to both the tree and woman. Root pruning would go a long way to solve this issue, unlike foot-binding. Even though a plant contained in a pot is considered unnatural, along with the practice of pruning its roots back to stop it from being root-bound, pruning remains the only natural means of allowing the plant to thrive in its natural habitat.

Take note of the way the roots encircle the pot. This marks the first stages of being root-bound. Within a year or two, the roots begin to thicken, and the space between roots shrink while the soil mass depletes.

What Are the Signs That a Bonsai Needs Repotting?

There are rules that reveal when to repot a tree. It is essential to know that for bonsai, these rules are mere suggestions since bonsais differ from tree to tree, place to place, and person to person. Some rules state that a bonsai should be repotted every two years or so. This depends on the kind of soil medium used.

The two-year rule was put in place because of *akadama,* a type of bonsai soil mix which breaks down after a few years since it is a type of clay. When *akadama* soil breaks down, it compacts and loses its super permeability. Again, while breaking down into little bits, this medium loses its ability to efficiently absorb nutrients. So you can now understand the origins of the two-year rule.

That being said, time is not the only factor one can use in choosing to repot a tree. Loads of signs exist, which can hint you as to when to repot your tree.

A very good sign is water.

How? Several times, when you water a tree, it sips immediately into the soil and drains out just as quick. Whenever you see signs that it's taking longer for water to penetrate the soil, it signifies that the roots and soil have compacted to a degree that could impact the tree's health.

Another good indicator is the root ball.

At the end of the two years, if the wires holding the root ball hasn't been cut, do so. Take out the tree, and inspect the root mass. Roots that encircle the pot will continue to encircle and thicken. With time, this continues and begins to hurt the tree because important feeder roots can't be sent out by the tree to receive its much-needed water. If the tree's roots don't fill and encircle the pot, it's a great idea to leave it and allow it to grow a bit more.

Which Period of the Year Is Perfect for Repotting?

By now, you are certain to know it's important to follow the rules of bonsai. Repotting, too, has a set time-frame rule that, honestly, should be loosely followed.

So what time can you get the deed done? This depends on the species of trees, but normally, a good practice is to repot during spring, even though tropical trees can be repotted at any time of the year. Yet again, it differs from tree to tree and place to place. It's really beneficial to spot the signs the tree shows you when it's ready to be repotted.

Spring is the general period to aim for. Yes, you heard it. It can be further divided into early spring, mid-spring, and late spring. For instance, your tree is ready to be repotted if it is root-bound and/or having issues with soil impermeability. Also, see it as a good idea to observe the tree in springtime to gauge properly if it is ideal to do so.

What's the Deal with Waiting?

The energy cycle of the tree is the reason we wait. This is also why we observe the tree in order to know, without errors, the most appropriate time for repotting. In order to read the signs properly, there is a need to understand how seasonal changes affect the tree.

In short, a tree loses its leaves to protect itself from harsh winter. Trees that hold on to their fleshy leaves will toughen up to protect their foliage during the winter, just like pine trees that are evergreen.

Having fleshy, broadleaf foliage is an indication that the tree is constantly using energy to keep these leaves lush in order to absorb sunlight to produce glucose. During fall, the tree sheds its lush, green leaves in order to store energy for harsh winter since winter freezes fleshy foliage. In winter, energy is transferred to the roots to store and use during the cold. When winter ends and spring begins, energy transfer can be seen when it moves from the roots above the ground and into the body of the tree to produce leafy, green foliage one more time.

Therefore, to gauge the best time to repot, the simple equation to follow is, *leaves=energy*.

The best time is NOW!

Spring is the best time, at the start of warming up. Observe your tree, and if you notice the buds that stayed on the tree, after all the leaves fell off, are perking up and swelling. Ladies and gentlemen, that is the perfect moment to carry out your repotting.

That is the moment a transfer of energy is taking place. Repotting this period without causing catastrophic damages to your tree is possible. Imagine repotting too early. You will be trimming away the energy stored in the roots, which will lead to the death of the tree or will leave it severely weakened. Some experienced hobbyists will admit repotting at the wrong time have led to the death of their prized bonsais.

Summer and Fall Repotting

Isn't it possible to repot in the summer and fall? Most mandates express that spring is the best time and winter is a very bad time. How about summer and fall?

It is rare for repotting to be carried out in the summer or fall, yet it can be successful if it's done by an experienced cultivator who uses the right procedure. During the summer and fall seasons, repotting can be done on any species. However, repotting done during the summer or fall will most likely have a different result from a repotting done during the spring. The question then is, what are the differences?

A late spring or spring repot is less nosy, as the tree is repotted to give emergency activity to address poor soil waste, soil compaction resulting in deprivation of oxygen, and possible parasite invasion. More often than not, a summer repot is the subtle removal of a tree from the pot into a bigger pot, where the point of the tree is balanced. New soil is then added to the pot to cover the current root mass.

Procedure for Repotting a Bonsai tree

Usually, the procedure for repotting is applicable to any plant species of any style. One determining factor is time and whether the root can withstand much pruning. So assuming this is mid-spring, the buds are swollen, and the bonsai tree has been in its pot for around four years, it should be prepared for another pot, as it's a great opportunity to repot.

Highlights of Female versus Male Highlights of a Bonsai Tree

Feminine	Masculine
Delicate trunk	Intensely decreased trunk
Smooth bark	Mature bark

Sleek and smooth branching	Angular branching
Some deadwood	Deadwood

Step 1. Choosing a Pot

Before repotting, a new home has to be prepared. And to prepare the new home, another pot must be selected. It is a necessity that the pot is the same size as the former pot. A bigger pot would result in the tree developing exponentially. In the event that the cultivator aims to have a bigger tree, a bigger pot must be obtained. Also, the tree must be nurtured accordingly.

Usually, choosing a pot for bonsai is a challenging task because this choice will determine how much the tree will integrate.

Indeed, selecting a new pot is a delicate decision. But can one say that all pots are pots? Not in bonsai. A cultivator's pot choice will determine the synchrony between the tree and the pot. Bonsai pots are used basically for aesthetic purposes. In this way, it is vital to understand the guidelines of pot choice.

Measurements: A general standard necessitates that the depth of the pot is equivalent to the breadth of the trunk after it's planted into the soil.

Masculine versus Feminine: As trees can be arranged into having sexual orientation highlights, pots can, likewise, be sorted into these two classifications. Since pot shape and depth decide the sexual orientation of the pot, it is essential to understand how to combine it up with your bonsai.

- **Rectangular Pots:** These pots are regularly connected with masculine trees (highlighting every characteristic recorded in the table). The one tree that fits the rectangular pot is a conifer as it commonly has an increasingly powerful trunk and mature-looking bark.

- **Oval Pots:** This pot shape can be related to delicate bonsai, regularly used to show a scene or in a group because it's extended to offer more depth.

- **Round Pots:** These are connected with delicate female trees. This pot shape can be used for the deciduous trees and conifers.

Shading and Texture: Bonsai pots are in a variety of textures and colors. These are also used to compliment the tree. However, although not as vital as the pot's shape, colors are the last touch to adding that final synchrony to a tree.

Whether the pots come glazed or not, it is great to know that glazing of the pot can additionally help to characterize the potential tree.

- **Colored/Glazed:** This is typically utilized for blooming trees to emphasize the unique characteristic of that tree.

- **Earth-Toned/Glazed:** It can be used for any feminine tree.

- **Non-Glazed:** It's a masculine quality basically used for conifers.

Step 2: Preparing the New Pot

When your pot has been chosen, the plant is prepared to make the move to its new home. The first step is to make drainage screens. The screens will enable water to drain while holding the soil medium back. A copper wire formed into the shape of a staple is what holds the screen in place. The thin wires jutting out of the pot's base are strung through the little openings to guarantee that when you put the root ball in, it can be affixed so that the tree and pot are bound together to prevent the tree from moving as it builds up its new root framework. The base of the pot is further secured with the biggest coarse portion of the bonsai blend. This will permit good drainage.

Step 3: Relocating the Tree to the New Pot.

It's critical to take a bonsai sickle or *kama* and circumvent the perimeter of the pot to remove the root ball. After removing the tree from its initial home, some of the root balls must be removed. The act of removing some root balls is called "root pruning." A minimum of 20 percent of the roots and not over 40 percent needs to be removed. This is often very effective in many plant species. Pines and junipers may vary in their requirement. The soil can be further loosened to uncover more roots to be pruned further. It's ideal to use a long pole-like instrument (screwdriver) to wiggle the soil to remove the material off the roots.

Step 4: Check the Angle and Find the Front

When prepared to put into the new pot, the little hill of soil you have prepared for the bonsai pot becomes possibly the most important factor. If you haven't picked the front of the tree earlier because it's an already-styled tree, you will have to find out which is the front.

The front of the tree is only a term to indicate what will be the face of the tree. The front of the tree usually refers to the side of the tree that is most appealing to the eye, in essence, the most beautiful part. When discovered, put the tree onto the soil, and squirm it into place. The objective is to ensure the correct angle is accomplished. Include more soil, and modify the tree again into the dirt hill to get the preferred angle.

Step 5: Fastening and Introducing Fresh Soil

The next stage is to refill the soil. Prior to adding more soil to the pot, the root mass must be attached by projecting wires. These wires will help fasten and tighten the tree. After this process, soil will be added to the new pot.

It is important to note that adding soil to the new pot does not mean just pouring a new soil into the new pot. It is ideal that a stick is used to swivel and ensure that the soil saturates into the root mass.

Step 6: Finishing

The repotting procedure is close to completion when the root ball is brimming with crisp soil. Now, it's essential to ensure all the dirt has been worked into the pot. To confirm that the soil has been worked into the entire root mass, you can make a clenched hand and delicately pound the side of the pot with your palm to settle the soil. This is to ensure that the root mass is ready to effectively support the growth of the plant in the new pot.

Step 7: Watering the Tree

The final step is to water the tree. The reason for watering is to moisten the roots. Knowing that new soil has been added, this watering process becomes another crucial stage of the repotting. The water must be drained out as it is being put in the pot simultaneously. Initially, the water being drained will be murky. Eventually, it will be less murky and clean, as a result of the continuous watering.

Repotting is something that any bonsai hobbyist should anticipate. It's an amazing time to know the health of the tree and fix any issues. This is the point where the tree's *nebari* can be made, and it can take a long time to form. Repotting a bonsai is calming and therapeutic to an extent, and can be an educative teaching tool for any individual who desires to understand the tree's cycle.

Chapter 12

Presenting Your Bonsai

The whole theory around the art of bonsai is aesthetics-focused. When growing a bonsai tree, each cultivator is meaning to pass on a specific appearance of his perfect work of art that will charm the senses of whoever sees it. It is also vital for each bonsai cultivator to discover joy in the manner in which a tree is molded and styled for himself.

The stylish intrigue and pattern of bonsai is similarly exchanged between the bonsai cultivator and the public, who will get the opportunity to appreciate the bonsai creation.

The style in bonsai isn't only ascribed to the physical appearance of the smaller-than-normal trees but also with everything else in Japanese culture. There is a lot more to it than being basically satisfied with the outcome. Every bonsai masterpiece will pass on the enchantment of training bonsai itself. Therefore, the essence of bonsai must be considered.

The imprints the Buddhist monks left on bonsai are, without a doubt, precious.

It is the Zen philosophy of life, entwined with bonsai, in such a way that the two end up inseparable.

The two major components the Zen philosophy which had the most effect on bonsai are known as *"Mono no Aware"* and *"Wabi-sabi."*

Mono no Aware

This term can be portrayed as "a sensitivity to ephemera." There is a wonderful feeling of awareness behind this term. This feeling of mindfulness for the temporariness of everything on Earth brings about harmony to the consciousness.

By understanding how delicate life is, one can figure out how to develop unity, peace, and balance in his words and deeds.

Wabi-sabi

Wabi-sabi is associated with raising an individual's awareness. This makes it similar to *mono no aware*.

Notwithstanding, these two terms have their differences. *Wabi-sabi* does not focus only on the temporariness of things, but it is also concerned with recognizing the "imperfect, temporary, and incomplete."

The idea of *wabi-sabi* is to explain that feeling of tolerating the imperfections and incompletion of everything in life. It is additionally about enjoying the sweet nostalgia, which enables one's mind to free itself from the hold of the ephemeral, because one can now embrace the excellence and beauty of imperfections.

Portraying these classic terms is sensitive, particularly when one who isn't an Asian native desires to comprehend the in-depth value of both terms, *mono no aware* and *wabi-sabi.*

Bonsai, a plant perceived to be both blemished and ephemeral, draws its strength and charm from these same characteristics. It is, however, the understanding of the ideas— *mono no aware* and *wabi-sabi*—that helps a bonsai cultivator to genuinely learn the principles involved in sustaining these tiny arts to a degree of expertise.

Your mind is able to understand the plain idea of a bonsai tree because of those sensitive emotions and unpretentious, sudden consciousness. And bonsai passes it's an idea across by setting off those generally uncommon emotions.

In order to reach out to those exact feelings and exceptional effect hidden in the Zen philosophy and the very essence of bonsai, below are the top principles one needs to follow.

Miniaturization

If one is to look at a normal tree, it is difficult to bring oneself to a sensitive condition of mindfulness. Be that as it may, one cannot resist being captivated by the charm of bonsai. It's like looking at a rare miniature tree instead of the average picture of a tree that we are familiar with.

As such, it is essential that the bonsai tree is of a suitably small size that allows it to fit into a little pot or holder.

The main goal after this is to keep the small size despite the fact that time is passing, and the bonsai tree, if allowed to develop in nature, would surpass its miniature size.

Proportions among the Various Elements

With regards to proportions in bonsai, the rules are really clear.

Each cultivator of bonsai should make an effort to achieve such proportions as the tree would have displayed in its natural habitat.

A bonsai tree ought to just take after the looks of a customary tree, regardless of the distinction in size and developing conditions.

It is through this very method that the level of awareness in the contemplator arises.

Symmetry versus Asymmetry

Numerous beginner bonsai cultivators are victims of the false belief that bonsai is expected to exhibit beauty as well as tidiness.

In any case, with regards to nature, its genuine beauty is not passed on as a result of its tidiness or symmetry. Rather, it is the asymmetry, the minor defects, the "normal" looks which captivate the mind and give the soul something to think about.

Hence, bonsai ought not to be flawlessly symmetrical, much the same as this isn't the situation with any trees in nature.

BONSAI

Absence of Traces

While gazing at the miniature trees, a person forgets to consider the hands that have crafted them, and this is one of the profound beauties of the bonsai.

It usually appears as though some wonder or special case of nature is unfolding right in one's presence. However, in order to obtain this impact, it is important that the bonsai nursery worker makes an effort not to leave any hints of his work on the bonsai creation.

A bonsai tree, in all its radiance, ought to look as though taken straight from the woods, so real, so legitimate, in light of the fact that this is the manner by which the ideas of *mono no aware* and *wabi-sabi* can show their maximum capacity.

Poignancy

As mentioned earlier, the exceptional emotion which is passed on by the bonsai can be said to be that of sweet nostalgia. The feeling of nostalgia is, however, interlaced with the feeling of magnificence, which the bonsai tree reflects upon its observers.

The feeling of nostalgia and magnificence are absolutely important with regards to the growing of bonsai trees since it is on account of these emotions that bonsai is such a stunning art and not merely a planting assignment.

The Importance of the Presentation of Bonsai

The manner in which a bonsai cultivator will present or display a bonsai tree is just as essential as every other aspect that makes up the bonsai masterpiece, for instance, shaping the trunk, branches, and leaves.

The standards of both *wabi-sabi* and *mono no aware* can be passed on by the bonsai tree gardener through an appropriate display of the tree.

The major reason for displaying a specific side of the bonsai creation is to show off the full excellence and skillfulness engraved in the art of Bonsai.

You can imagine the significance of this aspect, much like shooting film. If you are the executive producer of a film, you will be the one to pick the perfect angles for shooting the scenes in an ideal way. It is very similar to showing off a bonsai tree. Aside from the fact that, as opposed to picking the most suitable angles to shoot a scene, you pick the best angle to uncover the supreme excellence of your bonsai showstopper.

We have talked about the artistic beauty of a bonsai tree and referenced how important this aspect is. However, what is the depth of significance of the bonsai specimens' excellence?

BONSAI

With regards to the manner in which a bonsai cultivator will show the product of his efforts, the meaning behind the proper presentation of the miniature tree is connected to profound ideas obtained through history, much the same as with forming and chiseling a bonsai tree.

There are some key guidelines with respect to the manner in which the beauty of a bonsai tree will be displayed to its contemplators. Truth be told, the guidelines for showcasing the artistic beauty of a bonsai tree in its full magnificence are no less complex than the bonsai process itself.

The Front Side of a Bonsai Tree

The bonsai tree has a "front" side, which is viewed as more eye-catching than the opposite side, just like we have a most-loved profile of our face when we are snapping a photograph.

It is essential that the bonsai tree plant has the capacity to pass on the unobtrusive emotions, which will make the contemplators genuinely captivated by its charm. As such, all bonsai cultivators need to pick which side of the tree can best communicate the principal ideas regarding the bonsai magnificence and impact on the group of onlookers.

It is through this so-called front side of the bonsai tree that one can emphasize on the best angles of his bonsai masterpiece.

The Appropriate Height of Showcasing a Bonsai Tree

The position from which the smaller-than-usual tree will be viewed is essential. It is not just about picking the ideal profile of your bonsai art piece. The height, from which onlookers will view the smaller-than-usual tree, is just as important.

Take, for example, snapping a wonderful picture of yourself. Aside from having a better posture, the image should stress the emotion you wish to pass across to the people who will then see your image.

As such, if the image is captured from a low level (positioned close to the ground), the legs may seem slimmer and longer, among other features of the lower part of the body that will be changed. In the case where the image is captured from a high position, the facial features may be highlighted, rather than the whole body.

With regard to presenting a bonsai tree, the height from which you will display your masterpiece will affect the onlookers, as explained in the example of taking a picture. Thus, there is a need to choose the ideal height for displaying a bonsai.

In other words, it is entirely about harmony. Placing your bonsai masterpiece excessively low or high will destroy the entire effect. For this the reason, the cultivator will look for that brilliant bit of balance through the correct elevation in showcasing a Bonsai, which will trigger the feeling of taking in the genuine value of this old art. And just for that short period of gazing at the masterpiece, the observer forgets the customary world.

Emphasizing the Beauty of Bonsai by Removing All Clutter

The next thing after contemplating the "front" side of a bonsai tree and the correct height for situating the bonsai masterpiece so as to pass on the genuine effect of bonsai, there is one more factor which is of most significance.

The bonsai cultivator needs to consider the scene where the bonsai is to be displayed.

Taking the instance of snapping a photo of yourself, you know reasonably well that the scene will significantly impact the emotion and effect of the photograph. It is the same as in the case of displaying a bonsai masterpiece.

You must put in mind external factors as light, water, and wind, in the immediate environment, which will affect the impression of beauty, subtleness, and nostalgia of the bonsai leaves on the observers if it is to be displayed outside. It is, therefore, important to stick with basic, natural display properties, which include stones and/or wood.

After all has been taken into account, the bonsai cultivator must, by all means, avoid clutter. This refers to too much wind, light, as well as the scenery.

However, not only must the background be considered. The distance from which onlookers will observe the bonsai creation must also be considered. There is really no reason to become confused with the different rules that govern the correct presentation of a bonsai creation.

Much the same as everything in life, things are, in reality, a lot easier than they appear. You should simply keep in mind that bonsai is a work of art, and every art piece is best to be shown in a condition that is essentially free from diversion, have the perfect light, and the cultivator's interpretation in the right proportions.

A bonsai will better reproduce soul and plain emotions, which is to be passed on to the onlookers depending on how much it is free of redundancies, supplemental accessories, and, generally, clutters.

Increasing the Aesthetic Appeal of an Evergreen Bonsai

It is true that evergreens are not particular about the pot they develop in, as long as it allows for drainage.

Oftentimes, the perfect pot for evergreens possesses a depth of about one to three inches. It is, however, of utmost importance that the width of the container is suited to allow the growth of the evergreen bonsai's complicated root.

To stimulate new and healthy development, the evergreen bonsais should be repotted into new pots every two to three years. You could also add moss or pine-straw so as to improve the aesthetic effect of the evergreen bonsai, as such, creating a look of a natural forest though small.

Beautiful rocks, pebbles, and marbles could be included at the basal area of the trunk to create an admirable and eye-appealing scene. When assembled together to produce a small, dazzling, home garden, they could cover up all empty spots in the room.

From driving focus to the surfaces from which they are displayed to brilliantly enhancing indoor fountains, along which they are intricately placed, and to pricking the awareness of both the hosts and visitors, homes can be greatly improved with evergreen bonsais.

Conclusion

Start Growing a Bonsai Now

You definitely still have an interest in growing this master if you are still here. This book is the best book you can get on bonsai. Without a doubt, it is the most complete. All you are required to know is in it, and when I say everything, I am not joking about it.

By now you should be able to beat your chest to the fact that you can start to grow this world wonder right in your home. This art form is one that has been passed to us from many centuries ago. Therefore, you cannot afford to make it stop. The Japanese, Chinese, and the West are counting on you to continue the legacy.

Bonsai can be created from almost any shrub or perennial woody-stemmed tree species that produces true branches and can be cultivated in a pot confinement to remain small, after a series of crown and root pruning.

Bonsai teaches you patience and perseverance due to its long-term cultivation. However, it's worth the wait, as its beauty and appearance bring peace and harmony to whoever sees it. It brings humans to a state of awareness and mindfulness.

Made in the USA
Lexington, KY
14 May 2019